DATE DUE

5-22-96	

GAYLORD   PRINTED IN U.S.A.

Winning *with* Managed Futures

How to Select a Top Performing Commodity Trading Advisor

Thomas A. McCafferty

PROBUS
PUBLISHING

Chicago, Illinois
Cambridge, England

ISBN 1-55738-587-4

Printed in the United States of America

BB

1 2 3 4 5 6 7 8 9 0

CB

HG
6046
·M32
1994

In memory of John N. Knapp—
businessman, economist, philosopher

Table of Contents

Acknowledgments

As you read this book, you'll find constant references to the research of Barclay Trading Group. Its president, Sol Waksman, has been extremely generous with his time, experience, insights, and data. I can't thank him enough for his help and kindnesses.

The Managed Futures Association, headed by Jane Martin, was equally open and free with the enormous amount of information it generates. I strongly recommend its professional journal, *The MFTA Journal*, to any serious student of this industry.

My firm, Securities Corporation of Iowa, led by Eric Hender, has been extremely supportive. As were my fellow brokers—Paul Lovegren and Monty Wambold—who have contributed in ways they'll never know. Thanks also goes to David Knapp, who read the text for compliance purposes, and Doug Ramsey of SCI Capital Management, who prepared some of the research. Many of the illustrations were professionally created by Earleen Husman and Terri Cater of SCI's Graphics Department.

I'm also thankful to all the people within the managed futures industry who have been encouraging, helpful, and generous with information and advice—professionals like Lois Petz of *Managed Ac-*

count Reports, Dan Stark of Stark Research, Jeannine McGhie of BARRA/Mount Lucas Management, and Frank Pusateri of *Managed Futures Today*, to name a few.

There may be only one author's name on a book, but rest assured it is the work of many. Like the folks at Probus Publishing Company, who don't hold back anything to make their writers look good. Thanks one and all!

Introduction:
Why Search for a Commodity
Trading Advisor?

If you are like most erudite investors, everything you have read about commodity futures trading alerts you to the risk. Even in the sales literature touting its virtues, you find statements like: "Futures trading is a highly speculative investment, not suited for everyone. Past performance is not indicative of future results."

Yet you, like so many others each year, are attracted to the futures markets. The reason is often reports of nearly unbelievable returns from runaway commodity prices. In 1993, for example, lumber contracts soared over $200 per thousand board feet between January and March. That's a gain of $32,000 per contract in only one quarter. There were news stories in all the major media trying to explain why the move occurred and its impact on housing starts. What didn't get much coverage was the equally swift retreat lumber prices made. By May, they were approximately back where they had started. The wonderful thing about futures trading is that you can trade the bear moves as easily as the bull. If you had sold (shorted) lumber at its apogee, you could have rode it down for another $32,000 per contract of profit. The total would have been $64,000 in less than five months.

Your initial investment, called a margin deposit, would have been $1,200. This amounts to a gain of 533 percent, or a little over 100 percent per month! Did anyone actually make this kind of money during lumber's roller-coaster ride? We don't know of anyone and we doubt anyone could call this market that exactly. But we do know that many professional traders caught a good part of the middle of these bull and bear price rallies.

Obviously, there are three keys to the kingdom of futures trading—being in the right market, at the right time, and on the right side. Could you have done it—entered a long futures position in January, reversed at the high, and closed your short at the bottom? And this was just one of many serious market moves that occurred during this time period. Orange juice, palladium, Japanese yen, T-bonds, Value Line Index, New York Stock Exchange Composite Index, silver, gold, platinum, soybeans, soybean meal, and feeder cattle—all moved sharply higher. While corn, oats, pork bellies, wheat, copper, cocoa, and sugar traded markedly lower. Several markets traded steadily, neither gaining nor losing. Which ones would you have picked? Which ones would you have been long? Short? When would you have put on each position? More critically, how would you have decided to close each position? What analytical approach would you have used to make your decisions?

Even more critical to taking profits from futures markets on a daily basis is money management. The best traders preserve their capital for the trades with the most potential. How is this accomplished?

These are just a few of the questions professional commodity futures traders answer minute to minute, day to day. Then there is all the time and equipment required. Have you ever seen photographs of professional traders at work? They are usually surrounded by computers, modems, satellite dishes, fax machines, instant futures price quotation screens, time stamps, etc., etc. Most pay anywhere from $2,000 to $5,000 per month, just for the electronic gear needed to track prices 24 hours a day. Additionally, developing a computerized trading system can cost from a few hundred thousand dollars to millions of dollars.

Nowadays it's just about impossible to be a loner. A staff is a must—someone to do the bookkeeping, be sure the computers are blinking brightly, input data into the trading system, prepare documentation for government regulators, help to place orders, trade, and track worldwide markets, day and night.

The psychological side of futures trading must also be conquered. Speculating can be a cruel mistress. Sometimes you generate a spectacular profit from an error, by chance or without understanding why. Other times you carefully follow all your rules, take every precaution—only to be crushed! Not everyone adapts to the randomness of success or failure of these markets.

There are also years of study, practice, and apprenticeship needed to become a master trader. One of the common denominators we've noticed among all the top traders is their passion for the markets. They live, eat, and sleep it. If you visit their home or office, you are likely to find a quote screen in the powder room. Long hours, so they can cover the world's markets, are as common as corn in Iowa.

If you bought this book to learn how to hire a superstar trader, read on. That's exactly what we teach. As an extra benefit, you'll find out how an investment in a managed futures program might even reduce the investment risk you currently have, depending on the composition of your total investment portfolio.

Managed futures investments, in our opinion, are where mutual funds were a decade ago. With a small commitment to a fund or limited partnership, you can diversify your investment over dozens of futures markets. Additionally, you can have access to the best traders, who manage only large funds. These funds even further reduce risk, as we'll quantify, by using multiple commodity trading advisors (CTAs). We feel these investment vehicles are poised to make a major move. A careful reading of this book provides the information to make an intelligent selection. Best of all, you'll be prepared when the action begins—way ahead of the crowd!

Step one is to set some realistic goals. Chief among them should be the following:

- A noticeable reduction in the volatility of your portfolio
- The ability to generate a decent return under all economic conditions
- A globalization of your portfolio
- Marked improvement in the liquidity of your holdings
- The protection of investing in federally regulated financial instruments

It is our opinion that a carefully chosen futures trading program delivers all of the above. We also believe futures trading has grown so much in complexity over the last few decades that it is virtually a full-time business for anyone who actively trades. For this reason, we feel a managed futures program is the best choice for most investors who are suited to futures trading, unless they can devote the time and resources necessary to compete with the pros.

An Important Disclaimer

Futures trading in any form—be it an individual account or a managed program—is a very speculative investment. The risk of loss can be substantial. Not every investor is suited for it. Sufficient research, planning, and thought should be done before you commit funds to any futures investment. Always take the time to carefully read and study the disclosure documents, prospectuses, and offering memorandums of any managed futures programs you are considering as an investment.

Much of the information in this text was prepared from data obtained from hundreds of commodity trading advisors, CTA disclosure documents, pool prospectuses, and other sources believed to be reliable. Neither Barclay Trading Group, Ltd.; Probus Publishing Company; Securities Corporation of Iowa; nor the author made any attempt to verify any of the data supplied by the various sources for accuracy or completeness. You must also keep in mind, as you study the performance of the traders described, that their past performance is not indicative of future results. In most cases, the data represent a composite of all accounts a CTA manages. Any individual account may or may not show the same, or even similar, profits or losses.

All representations have been done for illustrative and educational purposes only. Nothing is this book should be construed as an offer to sell any futures program. Most managed futures programs can be sold only through disclosure documents, placement memorandums, or prospectuses.

Acronym Key

AP	Associated Person (Broker)
BNAV	Beginning Net Asset Value
CFTC	Commodities Futures Trading Commission
CPO	Commodity Pool Operator
CTA	Commodity Trading Advisor
DPP	Direct Participation Program
ENAV	Ending Net Asset Value
FCM	Futures Commission Merchant
IB	Introducing Broker
LP	Limited Partnership
NASD	National Association of Security Dealers
NFA	National Futures Association
POA	Power of Attorney
ROI	Return on Investment
ROR	Rate of Return
SD	Standard Deviation
SEC	Securities Exchange Commission
VAMI	Value Added Monthly Index

See Glossary, Appendix C, for definitions.

1

Recognizing and Using
Macro-Disqualifiers

The search for someone who can make money trading futures for you can be approached from two directions. First, what risk factors categorically disqualify potential candidates? Secondly, you need to develop criteria to guide you in the evaluation of the remaining universe of hopeful advisors.

We call an insurmountable factor that eliminates a futures trader from your short list a Macro-Disqualifier. A clear-cut example *could* be the country in which the trader or trading program legally resides.

Futures trading these days is done on a global basis, 24 hours a day. *The World's Futures and Options Markets* reference guide tracks price and trading volume history on over 600 contracts traded worldwide. There are now futures exchanges in over 25 countries. Here's a list of the top 10 exchanges, by trading volume, for 1993.

Exchange	Annual Trading Volume
1. Chicago Board of Trade	178,773,105
2. Chicago Mercantile Exchange	146,746,990
3. Liffe (London)	93,668,252
4. Matif (Paris)	72,263,961
5. New York Mercantile Exchange	55,412,436
6. B.M. & F. (São Paulo, Brazil)	52,263,719
7. London Metals Exchange	35,289,932
8. Tiffe (Tokyo)	24,121,713
9. Sydney Futures Exchange	21,481,096
10. Commodity Exchange Inc. (New York)	18,854,113

Notice that the United States no longer has a lock on the futures market. By last count, there were 62 futures exchanges worldwide, of which 47 were outside the United States.

This is a very important consideration because many of the best CTAs (Professional Commodity Trading Advisors) prefer to trade outside the U.S. and many emerging superstars are citizens of and based in foreign countries. Some countries, like the Republic of Ireland, offer excellent tax concessions and other help to financial service firms opening offices in Ireland, not to mention facilitating direct access to the European Community. The New York Financial Instrument Exchange (Finex), for one, has opened a new trading floor in Ireland. But the big drawing card is not financial incentives or lower costs; it is a more hospitable regulatory environment. Excess regulation in the U.S. drives investment advisors and trading volume overseas. For example, of the top 10 contracts by volume for 1993, half were traded on foreign exchanges.

Contract	Exchange
1. U.S. T-bonds (futures)	Chicago Board of Trade
2. Eurodollar (futures)	Chicago Mercantile Exchange
3. S&P 100 (option)	Chicago Board Options Exchange
4. Notionnel (futures)	Matif (Paris)

Contract	*Exchange*
5. Crude oil (futures)	New York Mercantile Exchange
6. U.S. T-bond (option)	Chicago Board of Trade
7. 3-month Euroyen (futures)	Tiffe (Tokyo)
8. Dax (option)	DTB (Frankfurt)
9. 3-month Euromark (futures)	Liffe (London)
10. German bund (futures)	Liffe (London)

The regulatory protection an investor may or may not have is a serious concern and can be a Macro-Disqualifier. In the United States, investors enjoy certain protection in the futures area provided by the oversight of the National Futures Association (NFA) and the Commodity Futures Trading Commission (CFTC). Individuals, companies, and other business entities must register with the NFA or CFTC to trade on the exchanges and do futures business with the public. If an entity violates any of the rules, the NFA and/or CFTC can restrict or terminate trading privileges—thus putting it out of business. Drastic measures like this are used only in extreme cases, but the regulators have many other less drastic remedies, such as fines, suspensions, etc.

The regulations govern sales procedures and financial requirements (capitalization), as well as trading. Certain individuals, such as convicted felons, are routinely denied registration, for example. All members and associate members are required to accept NFA or CFTC binding arbitration, if faced with a customer complaint. This is a fairly economical method of resolving a dispute. In other words, the regulatory bodies provide a formal procedure for handling any dispute you may have with a registered person or entity.

The financial integrity of your investment varies by country. Some take a very cavalier—*caveat emptor*—*stance, particularly when it comes to nonresident aliens of their country. Others are more stringent. In the United States, you are protected by the following safeguards:*

- *Daily Cash Settlement.* The market value of open futures positions increases or decreases in value as futures prices move up or down. Each position is priced at the end of each trading session. This is called mark-to-the-market. Gains can be withdrawn. Losses are deducted from equity in the account. If losses exceed equity, a demand, or margin call, requires an immediate deposit of additional money so that the proper margin or good-faith deposit is maintained at all times. Traders who do not meet margins are taken out of the market. Any debit is made up by the trader or the firm through which he or she is trading. This approach keeps all positions adequately funded, thus protecting your positions when you decide to close them.

- *Capitalization.* The CFTC and NFA require every firm in the futures industry to maintain a certain level of capitalization. The level varies depending on the amount and type of business conducted. Sufficient funds are required to meet the financial obligations that each firm has to its customers. The capitalization requirements are continuously monitored and stringently enforced. The regulators have the authority to determine compliance on a daily basis, if necessary, and demand, normally in very volatile markets, that additional capital be added with as little as one hour's notice.

- *Segregated Accounts.* Customers' funds and margin deposits must be held in bank accounts totally separate from those of the brokerage firm. Commingling of a firm's money with customers' funds is strictly forbidden. The money customers deposit can be used only for the purpose customers intend. Compliance with these regulations is strictly enforced and regulators can take immediate steps if they even suspect customers' monies are being improperly appropriated.

- *Emergency Transfers.* The regulators have the power to close a futures firm and transfer all accounts and open positions to a financially sound firm if they have any reason to believe a firm is jeopardizing the financial safety of its customers. This is done to allow the customers to orderly close positions and/or continue to trade without being forced to liquidate in an untimely fashion.

Two regulatory bodies, the NFA and the CFTC, were mentioned. The former is an industry self-regulatory organization, supported by a small fee charged to each trade executed in the U.S. futures markets. The CFTC is a government agency authorized every two years by Congress. In general, the NFA supervises the IBs (Introducing Brokers), who hire Associated Persons (APs). APs are brokers who solicit customers and introduce them to FCMs. FCMs are Futures Commission Merchants. They handle the actual trading in the futures pits at the exchanges. Your CTA or trading advisor transmits his or her order to a broker who, in turn, passes it on to an FCM's order desk at the proper exchange. The FCM order desk signals the trade to a floor broker in a trading pit. Once the trade is executed, the process is reversed. In fast markets, the whole process could take place in a matter of minutes. You or your advisor could still be on-line with your broker, after giving him or her an order, when the fill comes back.

At the end of the day, the floor brokers at the exchanges turn their trading records over to the exchange's clearinghouse, which balances all the trades. A detailed record of all trades by account, called the daily run, is wired (usually using a printer connected to a modem) to each introducing brokerage firm for checking. Corrections are immediately phoned to the clearing firm, which plugs the updated information in to the system. Trade confirmations are prepared by the FCM and mailed to your CTA. All this takes place before the next day's trading session.

If you are familiar with the securities industry, the CFTC is similar to the SEC (Securities and Exchange Commission) and the NFA compares to the NASD (National Association of Securities Dealers). (See Exhibit 1.1.) Also as in the securities business, participants in the futures industry are required to pass proficiency examinations and undergo a screening, which includes fingerprint checks by the Federal Bureau of Investigation, before registration can be completed.

The NFA also provides an excellent information service you should learn to use. You can call their toll-free telephone number (800-621-3570) and ask for the registration and disciplinary history on

EXHIBIT 1.1

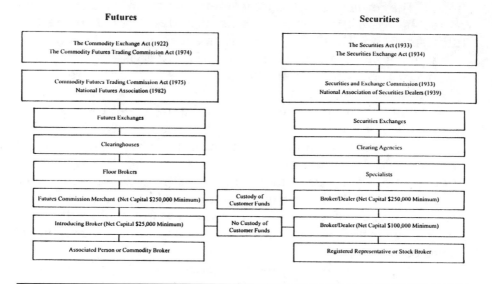

Futures		Securities
The Commodity Exchange Act (1922) The Commodity Futures Trading Commission Act (1974)		The Securities Act (1933) The Securities Exchange Act (1934)
Commodity Futures Trading Commission Act (1975) National Futures Association (1982)		Securities and Exchange Commission (1933) National Association of Securities Dealers (1939)
Futures Exchanges		Securities Exchanges
Clearinghouses		Clearing Agencies
Floor Brokers		Specialists
Futures Commission Merchant (Net Capital $250,000 Minimum)	Custody of Customer Funds	Broker/Dealer (Net Capital $250,000 Minimum)
Introducing Broker (Net Capital $25,000 Minimum)	No Custody of Customer Funds	Broker/Dealer (Net Capital $100,000 Minimum)
Associated Person or Commodity Broker		Registered Representative or Stock Broker

any individual or company registered in the futures industry. This should be one of the first steps you take to check out a futures industry participant.

Naturally, the United States is not the only country with a strong regulatory system. Most countries have security laws; even the National People's Congress of China recently passed some investor protection laws.

What you need to learn is what legal protection you have in whatever country your futures account will be traded. Compared to many countries, the U.S. is unique in that its futures laws are distinct from those regulating securities. Most countries lump them together. Also, the securities laws, which protect citizens of a country, do not necessarily give the same rights to aliens, particularly nonresident aliens.

This issue has become more and more important as more and more of the top CTAs set up shop in locations outside the United States. Some well-known CTAs, with hundreds of millions of dollars under management, have publicly stated they will not accept any more money unless it is outside the United States.

Another Macro-Disqualifier is an individual or a trading program that invests in a contract(s) that makes you uncomfortable. For example, one of the most important factors distinguishing one contract from the wide variety of other futures contracts being traded is price volatility over a specific period of time. The wider the swings from high to low on an interday, daily, weekly, monthly, or annual basis, the higher the associated risk.

Exaggerated price movement occurs for several reasons. First, there are some futures contracts that are considered thin. This means the trading volume is low. The lower the volume, the less activity it takes to increase volatility. It's like tossing a rock into a pond. The shallower the water, the bigger the splash. The same rock pitched into the ocean wouldn't even be noticed.

Pork bellies, platinum, shrimp, rice, cocoa, and cotton are some of the markets usually classified as thin. Refer to Exhibit 1.2 for a partial list of the wide variety of markets currently trading. Some traders specialize in one or more of the highly volatile markets because they offer the possibility of extremely high profits over short periods of time. Their trading strategy is to catch the big price moves that often occur. The wide market swings characterized by these contracts are more often than not reflected in the track record of this type of trader.

In other words, traders or CTAs who regularly trade the most volatile markets usually have the most volatile track records. They may be up one month 30 percent and down 40 percent the next. It takes a special type of investor to stomach these wild rides. As we'll see later, a portfolio of CTAs carefully blended together can absorb some of this volatility and make it more palatable. We'll also discuss how to measure and evaluate volatility.

When you read over the list of futures contracts, keep in mind that when you interview or study CTA candidates, it is important for you to understand something about the commodities they trade. Otherwise, you can easily be snowed into believing someone is an expert when he or she isn't. You'll be amazed at the depth of knowl-

EXHIBIT 1.2

Futures, Options, and Forward Contracts

Currencies

Australian Dollar	Irish Punt	
Belgian Franc	Italian Lira	
British Pound	Japanese Yen	
Canadian Dollar	New Zealand Dollar	
Danish Krone	Norwegian Krone	
Deutsche Mark	Portuguese Escudo	
Dutch Guilder	Singapore Dollar	
European Currency Unit (ECU)	Spanish Peseta	
Finnish Markka	Swedish Krona	
French Franc	Swiss Franc	
Greek Drachma	U.S. Dollar Index	

Metals

Aluminum
Copper
Gold
Lead
Nickel
Palladium
Platinum
Silver
Tin
Zinc

Interest Rate Instruments

Australian Bond	German Bobl
Australian Bank Bill	Italian Government Bond
Canadian Bond	Japanese Government Bond
ECU Bond	LIBOR
Eurodollar	PIBOR
Euromark	U.K. Long Gilt Bond
Euro Swiss Franc	U.K. Short Sterling
Euro Yen	U.S. Treasury Bills
French Notional Bond	U.S. Treasury Notes
German Bund	U.S. Treasury Bonds

Stock Indexes

CAC 40 Stock Index (France)
DAX Stock Index (Germany)
FT-SE 100 Stock Index (U.K.)
Major Market Stock Index (U.S.)
Nikkei 225 Stock Average (Japan)
S&P 500 (U.S.)
Tokyo Stock Price Index
Value Line (U.S.)

Agriculturals

Barley	Oats
Canola	Orange Juice
Cocoa	Plywood
Coffee	Pork Bellies
Corn	Rice
Cotton	Shrimp
Feeder Cattle	Soybeans
Flax Seed	Soy Meal
Live Cattle	Soy Oil
Live Hogs	Sugar
Lumber	Wheat

Energy Products

Brent Crude Oil
Crude Oil
Gas Oil
Heavy Fuel Oil
Natural Gas
Heating Oil
Propane
Residual Fuel Oil
Unleaded Gasoline

Other Indexes

CRB Commodity Index
Goldman Sachs Commodity Index

edge professional traders have regarding all the possible factors that influence the markets they trade. Additionally, traders need to be cognizant of both technical and fundamental factors, even if they only use one or the other to generate forecasts—either can move a market.

Your CTA must be prepared to protect your equity or take advantage of an opportunity when a major technical signal is hit or fundamental news comes into a market. Let's say your trader is a strict fundamentalist. He or she is poised to open a long position. Just before the order is placed, an important uptrend line is penetrated to the down side or a long-standing support price level fails. Your trader needs to know that all the technicians are watching this action and will respond bearishly. The thing to do is to wait until the bears feed before going long, if that is what your advisor's analysis indicates. Actually, if your trader is correct, it is an opportunity to get an even better (lower) price to open a long position.

Before we go much further, you have probably become aware by now that there is a variety of individuals and/or organizations that can trade for you. A commodity broker can. So can a friend, relative, or associate. If you select a registered commodity trading advisor, it could be a corporation or an individual. Therefore, we'll be interchanging these terms from time to time. Depending on your specific situation, the person who becomes your trader could be any one of these.

Let's briefly review some of the factors that influence the financial markets to get a feel for how complex price forecasting is. Any one of the following—and this is just a partial list—can drive the price of stock indexes, bonds, foreign exchange rates, interest, etc., higher or lower. Government reports on these indicators hit the market relentlessly, like the waves on the shore. Worse yet, the figures are constantly being revised, often drastically. You can make a trading decision based on a set of figures only to see a "correction" before you act. Here's the list of some of the fundamental factors:

- Inflation as measured by CPI and PPI
- Changes in business and/or consumer spending or borrowing

- Consumer confidence in the future
- Average work week in manufacturing
- Average weekly initial claims for unemployment
- Slowdowns in deliveries by vendors
- Contracts and orders for plants and equipment
- Housing starts
- Inventory adjustments and changes
- Changes in certain price-sensitive materials
- Stock and bond prices
- Money supply as measured by M1, M2, and M3
- Nonagricultural employment/unemployment
- Personal income
- Industrial production
- Manufacturing and trade sales
- Average duration of unemployment
- Ratio of deflated inventories to sales, manufacturing, and trade
- Labor cost per unit of manufacturing output
- Trade deficits
- Corporate profits

The list goes on and on and we haven't touched the technicals, such as cycles, the hundreds of price chart formations and thousands of permutations, relative strength indicators, speed lines, Japanese candlesticks, and so forth. With a sound understanding of how prices and price trends forecasts are developed, you can ask intelligent questions of CTAs and evaluate the answers. For example, going back to the example above, you might want to know

- What do you expect the Fed to do next?
- Which technicals do you rely on the most?
- When is the next *Beige Book* due out?

These questions lead us to the next consideration, which is the CTA's trading system.

Almost everyone who actively trades—futures, stocks, bonds, options—tends to be either a fundamental or technical trader. Both traders and investors have strong feelings about their approach to market analysis. And this is only common sense because in either case we're talking about foretelling the future. To accept another's forecast, or even your own, of what the price will be for gold, T-bonds, crude oil, interest rates, French francs, the rolling spot, or any other futures contract two hours, days, weeks, or months hence, takes faith. No one knows the future. We all accept that, yet we repeatedly ask people we trust for their prognostication.

Since the entire process of targeting price, or at least price trend forecasting, is an act of faith on the part of the forecaster and the forecastee, not believing in the method used by your trading advisor can be a Macro-Disqualifier. Experience has repeatedly shown there are times when the markets move against your most reliable prediction—yet you or your advisor continues to hold certain positions. When this occurs, can you be steady at the helm if you think technical or fundamental analysis is akin to reading goat entrails? Will you be able to discuss markets, act as a mentor, and provide encouragement in times of stress, if you don't accept your CTA's decision-making philosophy? When your advisor sustains an extended drawdown of your trading equity (and virtually every futures trader does at some point), can you stick with him or her if you are not committed to their basic outlook on the markets?

We stress this point because there are some very real differences, both psychologically and structurally, between fundamental and technical analysis. It is easy to find examples of cases when a fundamentalist and a technician study the exact same data at the exact same time, only to hear one come up with a very bullish scenario, while the other is bearish.

The reason for this is that fundamentalist analysts believe money moves markets and that money is committed to them logically. They rely more on the left hemisphere of their brain. On the other side of the aisle are the right-brain-dominant technicians. To them the markets are predominantly psychological. They study charts, ratios, momentum oscillators, etc., with the hope of anticipating where the herd will stampede next.

It is interesting to note that stock analysts are primarily fundamentalists. They want to know everything about a company—its markets, what the CEO has for breakfast, cash flow, competition, strengths, weaknesses, relationship to other trends and influences. The vast majority of analysts in the futures markets are technicians. Most of them are trend followers. They study price chart formations, Gann lines, moving averages, cycles, seasonal patterns, Elliott Waves, Japanese candlesticks, parabolic, speed resistance lines, and the list goes on and on.

There is a middle ground. Some futures traders study fundamental factors to discern long-term trends. Then they turn to technical analysis as a trade timing device.

The corn market provides a clear-cut example of how fundamental and technical analyses can work in tandem. This discussion also further illustrates how much basic information CTAs must have on the commodities they trade to avoid being blind-sided by an unexpected market-moving event or government report. First, you'll need a little background information. Corn is a member of the feed grains family, which includes corn, sorghum, oats, and barley. It is the single largest member and accounts for about 80 percent of the total U.S. production of feed grains.

The United States Department of Agriculture's crop year for corn begins on October 1 and ends September 30. Since corn can be stored for a reasonably long period of time and can be shipped long distances, tracking it worldwide is important and complicated. One of the key issues is usually pipeline supplies. How much corn is in farm and commercial storage (that is, left over from the previous crop years)? How much is expected from the current crop? Which countries are in need? More importantly, which ones can afford to buy on the open market? What government programs worldwide will increase or decrease production, imports, exports, etc.? Production and usage figures are constantly being compared to forecasts. The supply-demand equation looks like this:

Beginning Stocks + Production + Imports = Total Supplies
Feed, Seed, Residual + Food + Export = Total Usage or Demand
Total Supplies – Total Usage = Ending Stocks or Carryover

In the United States, the imports are not significant, since we produce so much. However, the export figure can make or break the market. If there is an abundance of inventory, it hangs over the market, depressing prices. If corn is scarce, prices soar.

Water is one of the most important inputs for grain production, making weather a key, yet totally unpredictable, factor. For example, corn requires 5,000 gallons of water per bushel. Eighteen to 24 inches of rain are needed during the growing season to produce 100- to 175-bushel yields. For every pound of dry matter (leaves, stalks, ears, etc.) produced, it takes 372 pounds of water. Normal rainfall during the growing season provides less than half the water, with the rest coming from subsoil moisture.

Water can be a problem at planting time and at harvest. In the Midwest, wet fields in the spring can delay planting. If it is substantially delayed, farmers can switch to soybeans, which causes corn prices to rise and bean prices to fall. Heavy rain at harvest can knock down stalks, slow harvest, and reduce yields. There's hardly ever a normal year—usually there is too much or too little moisture.

One of the most critical periods occurs when the plant pollinates. This period usually lasts for about 10 days around mid- to late-July in the midwestern corn belt. During this time, corn needs moisture. On the other hand, the temperature cannot be excessively high. A week of 100-degree-plus temperatures during pollination substantially reduces yields. Ideal growing temperatures range from 50 to 86 degrees. Beyond these limits, growth stalls.

As far as usage or demand is concerned, approximately 70 percent of the U.S. corn crop is used domestically. It is consumed as feed for livestock, food, alcohol, and seed. Feed is by far the most important. Demand, therefore, depends on the financial conditions of livestock producers and the cattle cycle. Are animal numbers increasing or decreasing? Are herds expanding or contracting? Demand for feed can be estimated when you can get a good fix on these numbers. The price of wheat and other grains must also be taken into consideration. Farmers will feed wheat as a substitute when it is profitable to do so.

The next biggest demand consideration is export. Although the U.S. exports only about 30 percent of its crop, this represents approximately 75 percent of the world's feed grain trade. Most countries produce their own feed, primarily in the form of silage. Only a handful of countries grow enough corn to be a real force in the export business. Of these countries, none are classified as steady and reliable suppliers.

In years when the fundamentals are clear and lopsided, forecasting is a snap. This, of course, is a rare situation. When supplies are tight, prices increase, usage declines (particularly exports to poor countries), and users switch to substitutes (livestock producers feed wheat, barley, or soybeans in place of corn; saccharin replaces corn sweeteners in diet soft drinks; gasoline displaces gasohol). If there is a plentiful supply of corn or demand is weak, prices move south or sideways.

If your CTA comes to the conclusion that the current overabundant supply of corn is about to tighten, driving prices higher, when does she or he institute a long (buy) position in the corn futures market? Your trader can draw a downtrend line on the long-term corn price chart and wait for prices to close above that trend line. The breaking of a trend line is one of the most basic technical signals.

Now what happens if the rise in corn prices stalls? Or worse yet, the downtrend reestablishes itself? This is where the fundamentalist and the technician separate company. The technician offsets the long position as soon as the newly developing uptrend reverses. The fundamentalist may continue to hold the long position, even if it begins losing money, as long as he or she is convinced the basic supply-demand equation has not changed.

Which works best in the futures market? Who is right? The only answer is the one who is successful in the long run. Either approach can work; either can lose money.

In one instance, if the fundamentalist is correct and corn prices dip, stopping out the technician, only to soar higher a few days or weeks later, she would be the hero. Or, if the fundamentalist's projections have been based on the continuation of a late summer drought that was unpredictably broken, she would be the goat.

This discussion of market analysis has nothing to do with what works or doesn't work. It has to do with understanding what you can live with or invest in and what you can stick with when trading becomes stressful. We've heard investors say, "I'd never have put my money with that CTA if I knew he believed in that malarkey!" In some cases the malarkey was fundamental analysis, in others technical.

Another Macro-Disqualifier is the type of program you back financially. The term "managed futures" can refer to any person or entity you grant authority to for the purposes of trading futures on your behalf. This could be a friend or a relative, a commodity broker, a professional commodity trading advisor (CTA), a private limited partnership, or a large public fund.

As a general rule, the more sophisticated the organization of the investment you participate in, the more legal and regulatory protection you have. For example, if you give trading discretion to your spouse's nephew and he loses all your money, what recourse do you have? Worse yet, what if he trades your account into debit, which means he loses more money than you put into the account initially, which you must make up? You can always try to sue him, but if he didn't do any wrong, except lose your money, you probably won't win.

As we move up the legal ladder, if you gave your broker, CTA, or other registered entity limited power of attorney to trade your futures account, that entity would be bound by all of the regulations of the NFA and CFTC. For example, the broker could not "churn" or overtrade the account in order to generate commissions. If you requested a written trading plan in advance and the broker violated it, you'd have recourse. The same is true if the broker misrepresented his skills, past performance, or experience. You could go to the NFA and ask them to intercede on your behalf. If you were wronged, you'd be compensated by the broker or his firm. Keep in mind that losing your money, even all of it, is not in itself justification for a customer complaint.

If you want to be sure your risk was limited to a specific amount, consider a limited partnership. With these types of investments, the investor's maximum loss is defined at the time of investment. This type of pool can be very small and private, or large and public.

The negative side of moving up the ladder is that the cost of investing increases, which means your investment dollars become diluted. For example, your spouse's nephew wouldn't even have to pay the $70 needed to register with the NFA, while the large public fund may expend hundreds of thousands of dollars in legal and regulatory fees.

Which is better? How can you evaluate the various opportunities? That's exactly what we're going to get into next.

2

Selecting a Baseline Measurement for CTA Success

"My CTA is beating the world!" That naturally is our goal when we select and invest in a professional futures trader, be he our spouse's favorite nephew or someone of the stature of George Soros.

In the securities market, measuring success appears to be reasonably easy. Most advisors evaluate their performance against the Dow Jones averages. Since beating the Dow has been the yardstick for trading success in the stock market just about from its first publication in 1884, let's examine it briefly and then see if there are comparable indexes available for the futures markets. But first, we need to understand the composition of the Dow so we can evaluate futures indexes.

How the Dow Is Calculated

Originally, the Dow was computed as a simple average—total up the prices of the stocks included in the index and divide by the number of stocks. Naturally, this system gave more weight to the higher-priced stock. Therefore, a major advance in a low-priced stock is diluted by a modest loss in a high-priced issue.

As the 1920s roared to a close, the stock markets were having a heyday. Prices were soaring and just about everyone in the country was buying on the cuff. To keep skyrocketing prices of hot securities within the price range of the majority of investors, many issues split, which caused some special problems for the Dow. For example, if one of the stocks included in the Dow was priced at $40 and split two for one, the day after the split it would be worth $20. The Dow would be artificially down. For this reason, the analysts over at Dow Jones introduced a flexible divisor, which is adjusted whenever an event (split, merger, major dividend) occurs that distorts the normal calculation by 10 percent or more. With the flexible divisor also came the concept of measuring the Dow in points, rather than dollars.

The key point of this discussion is that the Dow has been carefully modified, fine-tuned over the years so it can be used to measure the magnitude and direction of price movement over just about any period of time. Its weakness may still be the fact that, despite the flexible divisor, it is still price-weighted and can, therefore, give false signals.

There are many other stock indexes, some of which were developed to overcome the price weighting drawback. Take the Standard & Poor's Index as an example. To compute the S&P, you multiply the stock price of each underlying company by the number of shares outstanding. Then divide the total by the aggregate market value of all S&P stock from the base period (1941–43). The computation is then multiplied by 10 to get the index price at a specific time.

Stock gurus also have the Value Line, NASDAQ Composite Index, Wilshire 5000 Equity Index, New York Stock Exchange Composite Index, Amex Major Market Index, Amex Market Value Index, Russell 3000 Index, Russell 2000 Small Stock Index, and others as a baseline for measuring success. It's interesting to note that while short-term fluctuations often occur among the many stock indexes, the overall long-term trends are usually in sync.

The reason for this is that when we think of the stock market we generally measure success in terms of continuous price appreciation. Sure, one can sell stocks short, but it is not the common practice. The stock trader's mindset is to purchase a stock, hold it until it gains in value, and then sell—buy * hold * sell!

There are as many technical and fundamental approaches to stock picking as there are to selecting suitable futures trades, but the most basic is that the underlying company represented by the stock is making money. The more money it makes, the better managed, more competitive, faster growing, and more resistant to external factors it is, and the greater the dividend expected. Therefore, investors believe the Dow should continually rise. We measure our trading success against the rising tide of stock prices. Our expectation is for each company we invest in to become wealthier over time.

Futures contracts and futures trading are a horse of a different breed. For the most part, the commodities underlying the futures markets are simply entities. Grains, precious metals, petroleum products, food, fiber, money, etc.—they are stored or produced in anticipation of use. Prices are influenced by the ever changing supply-demand equation and the inflation rate. A commodity does not perform a service or produce a product that can be sold for a profit as does a corporation that underlies a stock, but the futures markets of the world nevertheless perform a valuable service for which they are paid.

Futures and options-on-futures exchanges sell price insurance, more commonly referred to as hedging. Producers and consumers of commodities can go to the futures markets and sell the risk of price increases and decreases to speculators.

Here are a few simple examples: A farmer plants a field of corn. He calculates his per-bushel cost—including seed, fertilizers, insecticides, herbicides, interest, labor, land charges, etc.—at just under $2.00 per bushel. At some point during the summer, the price of the December futures contract trades at $2.50 per bushel. The farmer is satisfied with a net before-tax profit of 50 cents per bushel, or 25 percent, on at least a part of his crop. He sells two 5,000-bushel contracts on the Chicago Board of Trade for delivery at a predetermined grain elevator in December. At this point in time, the farmer has locked in a 50 cents per bushel profit on 10,000 bushels of corn. He is long corn in the sense that he owns it because it is currently growing in his fields. And he is short, since he sold corn on the futures market. His only worry is not being able to deliver it when the futures contract comes due in December.

Or consider an inventory manager working for an electrical manufacturer whose bonus is based on buying silver at $5.00 per ounce or less. He needs silver, which makes him short the market. If silver is trading below $5.00/ounce, the inventory manager can go long the futures market and assure himself a bonus. He even has the option of accepting delivery of the physical commodity when the contract expires. Or he could offset on the futures position and buy locally on the spot or cash market. If silver prices go up, the profit from the futures offsets the higher cost in the cash market. If prices go down, the inventory managers lose in the futures market, but the cash market will be lower. The cost of his price insurance (the loss in the futures market plus the expenses involved in trading) would be compensated for by a lower per ounce silver price in the cash market.

A common complaint of anyone who buys insurance is that it wasn't needed—the house never burned down, the car never was stolen, etc. But few of us want to assume the risk that nothing unpleasant will ever happen, so we go ahead and buy the insurance.

The same goes for the futures markets. Hedgers buy insurance from speculators. A premium is paid for that insurance, which is the economic *raison d'etre* of the futures market. We'll continue this discussion and quantify the amount of premium hedgers pay a little later, when we review the various indexes available to you to evaluate your CTA's trading performance.

It's important to note that speculators do *not* create the price risk. This risk is there. It is real, whether there is a futures market in a particular commodity or not. As a matter of fact, price risk is substantially greater when there isn't a formal market. Open auctions with competitive bidding fixes prices. All the information—fact or fiction—affecting the perceived value of a commodity is resolved as buyers and sellers bid. This is true for the stock and bond markets as well as the futures markets.

If you ever have something you must desperately sell and there is only one buyer, you'll learn the hard way how the lack of competitive bidding hurts. For example, a farmer was heard to say at a very well publicized bankruptcy auction: "I'm glad all the sharks are here. Maybe some of them will eat each other as they circle me."

Now let's move from a market's passive economic return on investment—i.e., profits in the case of stocks and insurance premiums for futures—to discuss the concept of active asset management. How much does the skill of the trading advisor add to the return on investment figure? This also brings up the question of the randomness of any kind of price activity.

If the stock market is truly random, you should be able to compare the results of your advisors to those of the Dow or with another stock index that more accurately resembles your portfolio. If all your stocks are over-the-counter, perhaps the NASDAQ Index would be the best match. For portfolios of small stocks, consider the Russell 2000 Small Stocks Index. If your advisor beats the selected index, you should be pleased. If she or he doesn't, you naturally begin to wonder what you're paying for. If your advisor took you out of the market in September of 1987, you probably considered sending him or her a bonus as a reward for the skill or experience (or luck) displayed.

This discussion of the random nature of markets leads to a dichotomy: If the markets are random, does active management make any difference? If the markets are not random and there is a master pattern, why hasn't some extremely wealthy trader revealed the secret on his deathbed?

The discussion of the nature of the markets is as fascinating as the search for the Holy Grail once was. It is the meat and potatoes of the academic world. Open-auction markets result in real-world price discovery. They embody the collective opinions of the value of the stock shares, bond certificates, or futures contracts being traded. Prices mirror the herd psychology of the majority of bidders.

As such, they are sometimes coldly logical. This occurs when the supply-demand equation is clear. If the world is desperately short of oil, gold, money, etc., prices increase. They rise spectacularly fast because there are no sellers, everyone is a buyer. At some point, every commodity becomes too expensive and the bulls exhaust themselves.

Another face of the market is its Mona Lisa look. Is it happy or sad? Yin or yang? Bullish or bearish? The market cannot make up its mind to go up or down. The supply-demand situation is unclear. The supply may be known and adequate, but the demand is weak or coy.

When the market is logical, it is also reasonably easy to trade. The professional trader sells plenty of price insurance without having to pay out any claims. These are the markets friendly to trends-following trading systems. CTAs appeared to be clairvoyant.

The more emotional markets are also the more common. "Buy the rumor; sell the facts" sums them up. Guesses, misstatements, whipsawing price moves are the order of the day. Skill and experience are required to survive. More insurance claims are paid than premiums collected and a good many insurance companies (CTAs) go under.

Investors often ask why traders don't wait and trade when market activity is in sync with their trading system. Some actually do, but their trading volume is low and their investors become impatient. They want action, profits, above-average returns. It's not unusual for an investor to coax his CTA into overtrading. CTAs, after all, wish to please their benefactors.

More common are markets that appear to be calmly trending higher or lower one minute, only to be violently moving in the opposite direction the next. These events-driven markets are like shallow lakes hit by violent squalls. The bond markets are good examples because they are so responsive to good or bad economic news. Just a quarter of a point increase or decrease in the interest rates can send them soaring to the sky or down the tubes. The whisper of the word "drought" puts the grains in the stratosphere.

All these twists and turns, ups and downs, are graphically displayed by a variety of indexes. Some just give you the opinion of the majority of traders; others attempt to measure more sophisticated aspects of the futures market and its profitability. We'll review several of the more useful indexes now. It's important to understand how they are constructed in order to know how to use them to evaluate potential CTAs.

The granddaddy of commodity indexes is the KR-CRB Futures Price Index. The initials stand for Knight-Ridder Commodity Research Bureau. Developed in 1957, The KR-CRB Index was designed to monitor the broad-based price movement of the commodity market as a whole. It answers an important question, i.e., "Are commodity prices going up or down at any given point in time?" It is made up of futures contracts on the following commodities:

- Meats—cattle, hogs, pork bellies
- Metals—gold, silver, platinum
- Imports—coffee, cocoa, sugar
- Industrials—crude oil, cotton, copper, unleaded gas, heating oil, lumber
- Grains—corn, wheat, soybeans, soybean oil, soybean meal
- Miscellaneous—orange juice

None of the financial markets were included since they did not exist in the '50s. Since it does include physical commodities, which are so heavily influenced by inflation and deflation, bond traders love its inverse correlation with their market.

The KR-CRB Index provides an excellent insight into the overall price movement of the physical commodity market. In your analysis, you would compare your trader's performance in bull, bear, and sideways markets by matching his or her track record to the KR-CRB Index. Can you see a pattern? Are there specific types of market conditions that result in a disproportionate number of losses? This may be a Micro-Disqualifier, depending on frequency and duration.

Think of it this way. Commodities, particularly the physical ones, as opposed to the financial futures contracts, tend to be directly responsive to inflation. When inflation is increasing, normally so does the KR-CRB Index. Study the charts of the KR-CRB Index (Exhibit 2.1). Recently, from 1990 to 1994, we have been in a period of deflation. You can see that the KR-CRB Index has steadily declined. This is because the KR-CRB is heavily weighted to the grains, particularly the soybean complex. CTAs who trade the grains are good ones to analyze utilizing the KR-CRB.

You can get a better feel for the trading activity of your trading advisor if he or she specializes in a particular commodity group by comparing the performance with one of the KR-CRB's subindexes. Many CTAs offer multiple trading programs in specific commodity groups. You can invest in one that trades only foreign currencies or metals or grains—whatever. The KR-CRB Index has the following 10 subindexes.

1. Imports (sometimes referred to as softs or breakfast commodities)
2. Industrial
3. Grains
4. Oil Seeds
5. Livestock and Meats
6. Precious Metals
7. Currencies
8. Interest Rates
9. Energies
10. Miscellaneous

Another overall commodity index to consider is the GSCI, which stands for Goldman Sachs Commodity Index. It differs from the KR-CRB Index in that it is nearly as heavily weighted to the petroleum complex as the KR-CRB is to the grains. While both indexes are responsive to inflation and deflation, the KR-CRB Index often moves violently to unexpected events related to weather (droughts, floods, etc.) and the GSCI is sensitive to surprise political currents.

There is one other key to using these general types of indexes in your analysis. We refer to the concept of seasonal trends and cycle

EXHIBIT 2.1

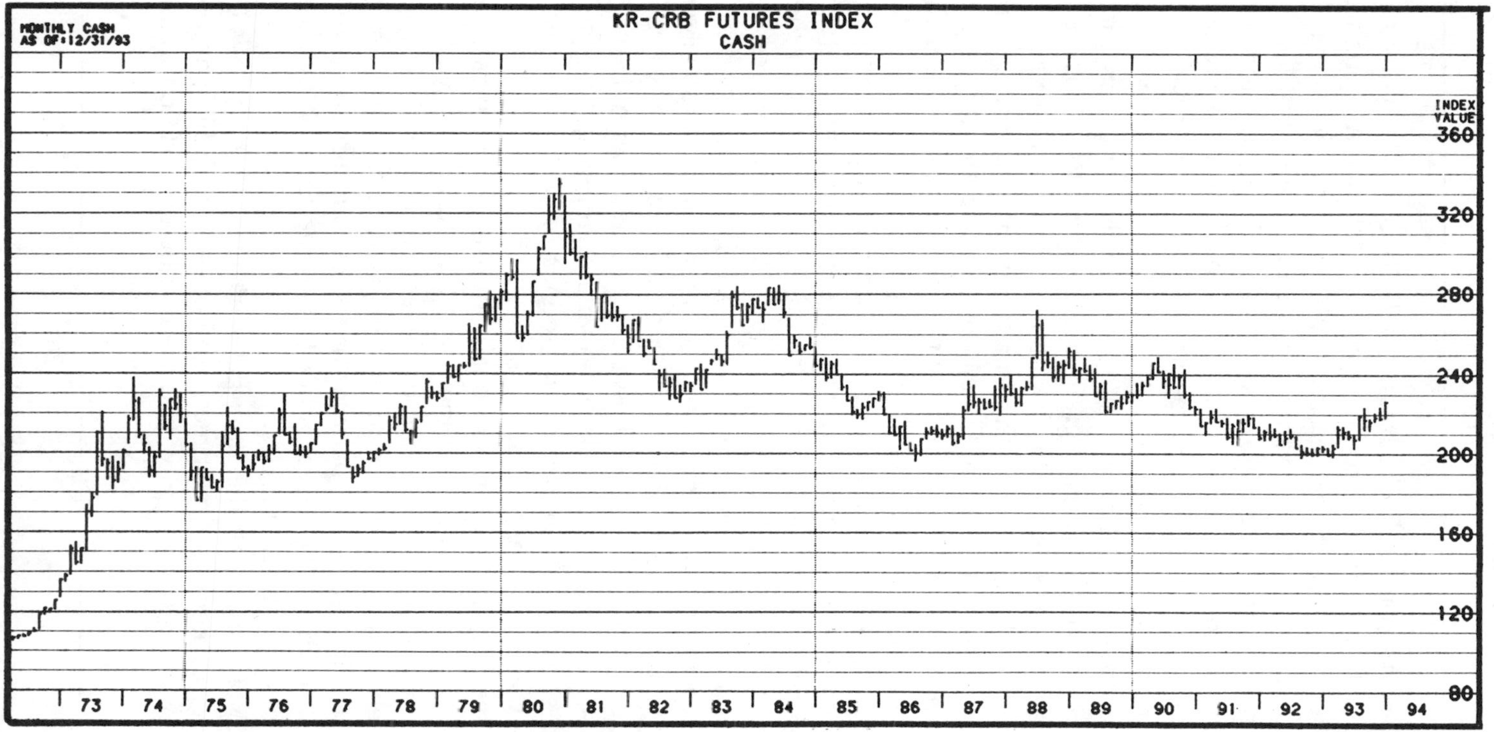

MONTHLY CASH
AS OF:12/31/93
KR-CRB FUTURES INDEX
CASH
INDEX VALUE
360
320
280
240
200
160
120
80
73
74
75
76
77
78
79
80
81
82
83
84
85
86
87
88
89
90
91
92
93
94

analysis. As you study the trading activity of CTAs, you want to be sensitive to how they negotiate seasonal patterns. Although all commodities have discernible seasonal patterns, the concept may be most easily explained via an example from the grain complex. The seasonal price pattern for a grain is simple. At harvest, there is a plentiful supply. Many farmers cannot afford or do not wish to hold on to their corn, wheat, soybeans, canola, etc. The marketplace is flooded with grain and prices are low.

As the bountiful harvest supply dwindles, prices are bid higher. Those who have stored the grain and accepted the associated risk of spoilage and price fluctuation want to be rewarded for providing this service to a hungry world. Eventually, the next season's crop begins to make its presence felt in the marketplace. If it is at least adequate, it has the power to halt or reverse upward price trends for the "old" crop, as traders wait for the "new" crop.

Seasonal trends are found by studying charts and comparing repetitive price movement to known supply-demand patterns. Gas prices increase as the summer driving season begins in the spring and early summer, as heating oil prices decline. Interest rates for short-term consumer loans inch up as Christmas approaches.

Experienced traders pay close attention to seasonal patterns. Many trade them exclusively. Once you begin to track a CTA, you need to become sensitive to how he or she deals with them. Another Macro-Disqualifier is a trader who *un*knowingly ignores well-established seasonal patterns because, sooner or later, that person will take a major and unnecessary loss.

Cycles are similar to seasonal patterns, but they can be longer than twelve months or extremely short in duration. Cycles are built on the observed phenomenon that events have a tendency to repeat themselves at more or less regular intervals. Much of human life is governed by repeatable patterns or cycles. Since humans made and control the markets, it seems fair to assume that the market would also possess definable cycles.

Cycles measure the time between each high or low (peak or trough). By knowing the time span between each high and low and the previous high and low, you are in a better position to anticipate the next high or low. Time is often measured in calendar days, as opposed to the trading days used by most systems. Calendar days are used for the simple reason that people and nature do not take weekends off—money continues to change hands and events affecting cycles continue.

A long-term cycle generally lasts a year or more, an intermediate cycle less than a year, and short-term cycles last a few weeks or days. As a general rule, allow approximately 10 percent leeway in the length of a cycle when establishing your expectation for the next top or bottom. Understanding cycles is just another key to evaluating CTAs.

It is interesting to note that both the KR-CRB and the GSCI can be traded on the futures market, just as the S&P or Value Line indexes. Some CTAs or trading programs specialize in strictly trading indexes.

While the KR-CRB and the GSCI provide an excellent insight into the direction the futures markets are trending and how a CTA deals with changing markets, they are of little help when it comes to evaluating how well a CTA is doing compared to the overall market or his or her peers. One of the reasons is that by its very structure and trading rules, it is as easy to short the market (profit from downtrending prices) as it is to go long. Secondly, futures contracts don't pay dividends. Nor do they have an indefinite life span, as do stocks in corporations. Commodities are not expected to generate profits by producing and marketing products or services.

As mentioned earlier, the futures market does provide a very important service, i.e., price insurance, for which it is paid. At this point, we'd like to quantify the amount of premium paid by hedgers to speculators for providing price insurance. To put it another way, it is the amount of return paid for assuming the risk of holding a commodity for future sale or delivery.

Some analysts also count interest income earned by a commodity account as part of the total return because a large percentage of the actual funds in an account lies idle at any given time. Sound money management dictates that 50 percent or more of the available equity be held in reserve. Some large accounts invest 100 percent of their equity in T-bills, only breaking a T-bill to meet a margin call. The interest rate the margin money earns is usually around the three-month T-bill rate or the current money market funds rate. Therefore, if T-bills are at 3 percent and a CTA's annual return is 25 percent, you may want to attribute no more than 23.5 percent to the efforts of the CTA. That's 3 percent interest income on 50 percent of the trading equity. On the other hand, if the brokerage firm you're opening your account with does not pay any interest, it could be a Macro-Disqualifier as far as using that particular brokerage firm. We'll get into fees and commissions later.

But what about the insurance premium the market pays the speculator? How much is it? How can it be determined?

BARRA/MLM Index

BARRA/Mount Lucas Management Corporation of Princeton, New Jersey, is a CTA and investment management firm. More important, it is one of the leading think tanks in the managed futures industry. What they've done is quantify the return that is built into the futures market, just as there is a return factor generated by corporate profits built into the stock market. Taken to its logical conclusion, MLM's theory suggests that managed futures are an asset class that provides an expected rate of return over long periods of time. It further suggests that a manager's skill or ability to add value should be considered only to the extent that the manager has actually outperformed the inherent return.

The MLM Index is calculated using a long-term, trend-following trading system. An algorithm signals when the trading system is to go long or short each of the futures markets included in the index. The positions are held on an unleveraged basis, which means the investment is equal to the face value of the futures contract in the index. Thus the index can be used as a fair comparison to cash-type indexes, such as stocks, bonds, and real estate. Additionally, the BARRA/MLM Index includes the interest that would be earned by the excess margin money held in short-term government securities, plus the capital appreciation gained by the futures trading.

The trading signals that toggle the investment from a long position to a short position and back again are completely automatic. There is no management. This is a totally passive approach to futures trading. It was specially done this way to take the skill, the experience, and the special knowledge of the CTA out of the equation. The objective is to capture only the innate value inherent within the futures markets. It is the amount of money the hedger is willing to pay the speculator for accepting the risk of holding a commodity while its price fluctuates.

We'll go into a little more detail regarding this index for two reasons. First, it will give you confidence the structure has been well conceived. Secondly, you need to understand how the index was created to be able to compare it with similar indexes, such as the Dow Jones Averages, Salomon Brothers Corporate Bond Index, the Frank Russell Company's Indexes, the S&P, and others.

First, let's consider how the specific markets and futures contracts are selected. Only highly liquid U.S. futures markets are currently included in the index; the choice of markets for a calendar year is made in the December preceding the start of the year and markets are not added or deleted from the index during a year. If a commodity is traded on more than one futures exchange, only the one with the largest open interest is included. For example, Chicago Board of Trade wheat has larger open interest than Kansas City Board of Trade wheat; consequently, Chicago Board of Trade wheat is included in the index but Kansas City Board of Trade wheat is not.

As mentioned earlier, the system just automatically toggles from a long to a short position and back again to remove any implication of a trader's skill. The index captures the return inherent within the futures market, as the Dow captures the return generated by a group of unmanaged stocks.

The rate of return of an individual futures market depends on whether the market position is long or short. Since a futures contract eventually expires, the index is based on the unit asset value of a market, rather than on the actual futures price. It is a similar approach to the way stocks are evaluated on the Dow. This month's unit asset value of a futures market is determined by multiplying last month's value by 1 plus the percentage change in this month's nearby futures price. The market position is long during the current month if the market's closing value of the prior month is greater than or equal to the market's 12-month moving average of closing value; otherwise, the market position is short.

A market's 12-month moving average of closing values is defined as the average of the 12 closing unit asset values of the 12 months immediately preceding the beginning of the current calendar month. For example, to find the 12-month moving average for June 1995, first find the unit asset value for the last trading day of each of the prior 12 months, June 1994 through May 1995. The average of those 12 values equals the 12-month moving average.

If the market position is long, then the market monthly rate of return equals the percentage change in the market price during the month, i.e., the market monthly rate of return (percent) equals the closing price of the current month divided by the closing price of the prior month, minus 1, times 100. If the market position is short, then the market monthly rate of return (percent) equals –1 (minus one) times the percentage change in the market price during the month, i.e., the market monthly rate of return equals the closing price of the current month divided by the closing price of the prior month, minus 1, times –100 (minus 100). The rate of return for each individual market is added together and a simple average is calculated to arrive at the monthly rate of return for the index as a whole.

The only thing left to do is convert the monthly average to an index equivalent. This is done by compounding the index monthly rates of return. The beginning value of the index is defined to be 1000 in January 1961. Each month thereafter, the index is changed by the monthly rate of return. That is, each month's index value is determined by multiplying the prior month's value by 1 plus the current percentage monthly rate of return. A chart of the index can be found in Exhibit 2.2.

Not everyone agrees with this theory in its entirety. Some observers, while agreeing in principle that a risk premium is providing an underlying return, hold that managed futures are first and foremost a *skill class* rather than an asset class. They argue that the disper-

EXHIBIT 2.2

Empirical Evidence of Returns: The BARRA/MLM Index

- **Definition:**

  The BARRA/MLM Index is a recognized benchmark for managed futures performance. The BARRA/MLM Index shows the returns, inclusive of interest income, available to a naive investment program. The index does not utilize leverage, is capitalized equally across all markets, and is completely idependent of manager-specific skill.

- **Historical Results:**

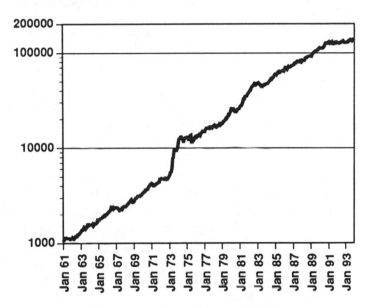

Compound Annual Return = 16.15%
Standard Deviation of Annual Returns = 18.41%

sion of returns among individual managers in the managed futures sector is so great as to minimize the apparent value of the inherent return. In fact, the average intercorrelation among the fifty largest CTAs, as calculated by the Barclay Trading Group, over the past three years equals +0.197. This low intercorrelation corroborates the dispersion of returns argument.

Proponents of the skill class theory also point out that unlike traditional equity managers who take only long positions, CTAs typically derive profits from both long and short positions. As a result, their total return may be highly uncorrelated with the performance of the underlying asset class (e.g., the physical commodity or financial instrument). While not disagreeing with the idea that the hedger's "risk premium" could benefit both long or short positions, these observers take issue with the picture of an industry dominated by flexible long-and-short position takers who are defined as an asset class. Instead, they suggest that the individual CTA adds significant value to the money management process and that the skill portion of a total return is at least as important as the inherent return.

Other skeptics argue that managed futures returns—and, in many cases, all trading returns—are largely the result of luck. These skeptics describe managed futures trading as a black box that offers no long-term expected return. They further suggest that a manager's prior returns are of little value in predicting future success.

This criticism, when solely leveled against the managed futures industry, seems unfair. *The Wall Street Journal*, a staunch supporter of the general securities industry, regularly runs a feature in its "Money and Investing" section. It pits top stock pickers against a portfolio of securities randomly selected by throwing darts. As often as not, the randomly selected stock portfolios outperform the analysts. Or consider the fact that two-thirds of mutual funds underperform the Dow. Despite these results, no one insinuates that stocks are not an asset class and that the analysts are.

To us, the debate is academic. We're pragmatists. There are financial analysts that regularly outperform the Dow, as there are CTAs that do substantially better than the BARRA/MLM Index. We don't care if the stock and futures markets are random or not. Our objective is to assist you in finding and evaluating traders who can achieve outstanding results.

So far, you should have a good understanding of how to look at the overall trends of the futures markets via the KR-CRB. This gives you a feel of how a potential trading advisor performs in bull and bear markets. Next, we saw how to judge the minimum return a trader should generate given the futures markets innate economic value. It's now time to begin to learn how to evaluate the skill and experience of potential CTAs.

3

Beginning the CTA
Evaluation Process

One word you almost get tired of hearing as you study the futures markets and search for qualified traders is *volatility*. We've already touched on why certain extremely volatile markets should be viewed with caution. The same goes for very volatile CTAs. Unless you are prepared—psychologically and financially—for very wide swings from positive to negative returns from one month to the next, a highly volatile trading record can be a Macro-Disqualifier. What we're talking about is a trader who gains 20 percent one month and loses 15 percent the next, or vice versa.

To thoroughly understand this concept, we must talk a little about the law of probability and the concept of standard deviation from the mean. These are some of the concepts we'll eventually use to select the CTA or trading advisor with the best chance of making money.

Markets (stocks, bonds, futures, etc.) move randomly. Sometimes they trend up or down with what appear to be logical reasons, but most of the time no one can, with any certainty, tell us what tomorrow's prices will be. Just when you think IBM will rise forever, you learn they misjudged the personal computer market. Or when you're convinced inflation is whipped and bond prices are headed higher, the Federal Reserve intervenes with an unannounced quarter of a percent interest rate hike—tanking them! Or all your research indicates soybean stocks worldwide are growing, only to learn the South American crop has been devastated by a drought or a flood. Unexpected events—be they natural disasters, political, social, or economic—occur with enough regularity to make you a believer in keeping the law of probability at your back.

Qualifying Random Price Activity

The following is an abbreviated version of the discussion of volatility from Sheldon Natenberg's *Option Volatility & Pricing: Advanced Trading Strategies and Techniques*. If you feel you need more detail, we recommend this work highly. As he explains, extensive experimentation has documented that no matter how many times you flip a coin, there is always a 50–50 chance of getting a head or a tail. If you flip a silver dollar 100 times and get 99 straight heads in a row, you still have only a 50–50 chance of getting a head on the one-hundredth toss.

This is the bedrock on which the concept of normal distribution of random events is built. For example, flip that silver dollar 225 times, or 15 separate series of 15 attempts each. As you repeat this experiment over and over, you may or may not get the exact results illustrated. Nevertheless, the results will fall into a predictable pattern, similar to the following:

Series Results	#Heads	#Tails
1	1	14
2	2	13
3	3	12
4	6	9
5	8	7
6	7	8
7	10	5

Series Results	#Heads	#Tails
8	11	4
9	9	6
10	5	10
11	6	9
12	4	11
13	2	13
14	1	14
15	0	15

Assuming you are using a balanced coin, you'll learn that the results most often occur in the middle of the spectrum. It would be very unusual (32,000:1) to get all heads or tails. Or only one or two tails and the rest heads. Normal distribution describes that which is likely to happen with random events. Charting this on a graph produces a bell-shaped curve. The bell-shaped curve graphically describes the distribution curve. The one produced by tossing a coin repeatedly is known as "normal" or moderate in appearance, but the shape can change. Widely spread data produce flat arcs because the data points are scattered. Data representing a CTA whose monthly returns are very consistent results in a curve that is very steep or narrow, since the data points are close together. (See Exhibit 3.1.)

You need to come away from this discussion with an understanding that the flatter the shape of the distribution curve, the more volatile is the data being analyzed, such as the monthly ROR of a CTA or trading program. Our objective is to quantify volatility. Once this is done, we will begin to make statistically valid estimates of a CTA's level of risk.

Stamp the words "statistically valid estimates of the risk that can be expected" on your wrist. This is the best you can do when you are attempting to forecast trading success. On average, or normally, you'll be correct. This doesn't mean you'll be right all the time or even half the time. You'll still be wrong some of the time.

What it does do for you is put the odds for success in your favor—giving you an edge. You have a new way of looking at CTAs and an excellent insight into a trader's volatility, allowing us to answer questions such as:

EXHIBIT 3.1

Volatility Curves

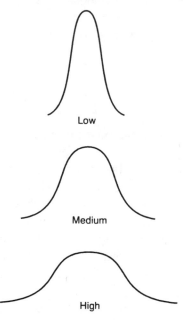

The closer price points are, the lower the volatility of a CTA or a managed futures trading program. Highly volatile traders are characterized by wide or flat curves, since the data points are more spread out.

Source: Russel R. Wasendorf and Thomas A. McCafferty, *All About Options,* Chicago: Probus Publishing Company (1993), p. 72.

- How wild a trader is this person?
- What are the chances he or she will be blown totally out of the market?
- Am I comfortable with this much (or little) activity?

It is important to note that volatility analysis of this sort is colorblind. The bell curve quantifies how wide the distance is between data points, which are usually monthly return-on-investment figures.

It doesn't care if the numbers are all positive, all negative, or a combination. There are a few CTAs with high volatility monthly rates of return that rarely have a losing month. A trader like this may move from being up 50 percent one month to being up 5 percent the next. If this is the case, we are less concerned about the degree of volatility. The more common situation involves swings from the positive to the negative side of the ledger. This is when volatility becomes one of our prime concerns.

The second part of this discussion deals with the concept of standard deviation from the mean. First, the mean is simply the average of the data and the peak of the bell curve. The standard deviation describes the arch of the curve. You can define it as the square root of the average of the squared deviations of the monthly rates of return from the arithmetic mean rate of return. The standard deviation measures the average or normal spread of monthly returns around the mean. Flat curves represent trading programs with high volatility; steep or narrow curves reflect low volatility, meaning the CTA is consistent.

For purposes of illustration, we'll go back to our coin-flipping example of making 15 series of 15 flips each. To find the mean, you multiply the number of either heads or tails (only one side need be calculated) in each flip by the number of that flip and divide the total by the total number of heads (occurrences) recorded.

Flips	×	# Heads		
1	×	1	=	1
2	×	2	=	4
3	×	3	=	9
4	×	6	=	24
5	×	8	=	40
6	×	7	=	42
7	×	10	=	70
8	×	11	=	88
9	×	9	=	81
10	×	5	=	50

Flips	×	# Heads		
11	×	6	=	66
12	×	4	=	48
13	×	2	=	26
14	×	1	=	14
15	×	0	=	0
TOTALS		75		563

$563 \div 75 = 7.5067$

The mean or average for 15 coin flips is 7.5, which is logical, since we expected the normal flip of a coin to be a 50–50 proposition. Therefore, approximately half the data points would fall on each side of the bell curve if we were to plot the results.

Calculating the standard deviation is somewhat more involved, utilizing very complex algebraic formulas, which Mr. Natenberg discusses in detail in his work. All most investors need to know is how to evaluate performance by comparing the standard deviation of one CTA to that of another. In our coin-flipping example, the standard deviation calculates to approximately 3.00. Standard deviation tells us two things about the data: first, how scattered or diverse it is, and second, the probability of any specific outcome. In the case of a CTA, pool, or fund, you can *estimate* the anticipated rate-of-return range within which the trading program normally falls at the end of each trading period, usually a month.

You need not worry about not being able to calculate the standard deviation. Any investor who uses it regularly nowadays relies on computer programs. The function for calculating it is built into most advanced spreadsheet programs. You simply key in the monthly rates of return and call up the standard deviation function. The computer does the rest.

Normally, what is done is to generate more than one standard deviation. It is common to figure one, two, and three standard deviations from the mean. These standard deviations are on both sides (plus and minus) of the mean. They tell us what percentage of the occurrences (monthly rates of return) being evaluated fall on either side of the mean. Here's the guideline:

- Plus or minus one standard deviation includes 68.3 percent, or two-thirds of all occurrences.

- Plus or minus two standard deviations includes 95.4 percent, or 19 out of 20 occurrences.

- Plus or minus three standard deviations includes 99.7 percent, or just about all occurrences.

This simply means that if the result we are expecting, known as occurrences, falls within one standard deviation of the mean (average or midpoint of the bell curve), we would have a two-out-of-three chance of that happening. Don't forget this is plus or minus one standard deviation, which means the result could be positive or negative.

Let's say you wanted to know the probability of a certain CTA's monthly rate of return "averaging" 3 percent per month. By running a standard deviation of previous monthly rates of return, you could calculate the probability of that happening. But is there some "Kentucky windage" involved? Do you use all data available, even if the CTA has modified his or her trading system? Or what if he or she is no longer trading the same commodity group(s)? If the CTA has a long record, is the last 12 months more or less important than the previous 36?

Does the use of standard deviation guarantee predictable results? Definitely not! Nothing is for sure when it comes to investing or forecasting future occurrences. Even at the third deviation level there is a 0.3 percent chance that the next occurrence will be outside the range.

To get back to our coin-flipping example, the mean is 7.5 and the standard deviation is 3. Therefore, the first standard deviation ranges from plus or minus 3 of 7.5, or from plus 4.5 to minus 4.5. This would be a line (refer back to our table of results) between Flips #4 and #5 and Flips #10 and #11. Therefore, all the combinations of coin flips from 5 through 10 would have a two-thirds probability of happening. If we were to flip a balanced coin from now until eternity, the law of probability states that 68.3 percent (approximately two-thirds) of the results would fall within this range.

Now let's get back to managed futures analysis. What we will be doing is taking a snapshot of the current trading activity and making some projections. When we do this, there are three things that can go awry. First, even if we use the third standard deviation, there is a 1 in 369 chance the next data point will be outside the parameters. Second, we could anticipate a positive move and actually experience a negative one. In other words, our estimation of the results expected could be incorrect. Third, we could be using an incorrect volatility figure.

The volatility value changes whenever a new data point is added. The change may be virtually immeasurable if the new data point falls near the mean, but it occurs nonetheless. It is for this reason we think of our analysis as a still photo of an ongoing process. Underline the word *process*, since evaluating CTAs is indeed a long-term process. When each piece of new data becomes available, the computer program should be rerun and the analysis process grinds forward.

Rating CTA Volatility

You can use volatility as a filter in your CTA selection process. As an example, let's review a study the Barclay Trading Group conducted on their CTA database. It classified CTAs by their level of volatility (high, medium, low) and then determined which group was the best investment.

The CTAs chosen to be included in the study all had trading programs with at least three years of performance history and $5 million under management. This resulted in a total population of approximately 136 CTA programs.

First, they ranked all 136 programs from highest to lowest by the standard deviation (SD) of their monthly returns, then separated the total group into three categories. The top third—i.e., those having the highest standard deviations and hence termed the "high-volatility group"—had SDs above 8.59 percent per month. The middle third, or "medium-volatility group," had monthly SDs between 5.31 percent and 8.59 percent. The bottom third, or "low-volatility group," had monthly SDs less than 5.31 percent. Within each of the three categories, Barclay ranked the programs by their compound annual return.

They used standard deviation of monthly returns to determine the three performance categories for two important reasons. First, standard deviation is a good measure of the consistency or variance of returns. It is generally not unduly skewed by a few outlying data points.

Second, standard deviation of monthly returns is not *per se* a judgment as to the "goodness" or "badness" of a CTA's performance. A low-volatility trader could have very consistent returns figures and be losing money. On the other hand, it's possible for a CTA to have a very high standard deviation of monthly returns and also have no losing months, assuming that all returns were positive.

The objective of this type of exercise is to categorize CTAs based on the consistency of their returns and to apply other parameters to determine which ones are the superior traders. The results are summarized in Exhibit 3.2.

As one might expect, the top performers in the high-volatility group had the highest compound return, an average 42.30 percent. The medium-volatility group averaged 29.73 percent, while the low-volatility CTAs were at 15.80 percent. The worst drawdown results are also as expected—the high-volatility CTAs averaging 28.90 percent and the low-volatility category only 8.50 percent.

The results are even more interesting when we look at the reward-risk comparisons for each group. This is done by dividing the average monthly returns by the SD of the monthly returns. Obviously, the higher the ratio the better, given a rational investor's desire for high rates of return combined with low variability of returns. By this measure, the low-volatility CTAs offer a reward-risk profile that

EXHIBIT 3.2

Average Performance of Top 20 CTAs in Three Volatility Categories
for the Period 10/1/89 to 9/30/92

Volatility Category	Std. Deviation of Monthly Returns	Compound Annual Return	Worst Drawdown	Avg. Monthly ROR/SD Return	Three-Year Compound Ret/ Worst Drawdown
High-Volatility	>8.59%	42.30%	28.90%	.312	1.46
Medium-Volatility	5.31% – 8.59%	29.73%	18.44%	.330	1.61
Low-Volatility	<5.31%	15.80%	8.50%	.433	1.86

Source: Barclay Trading Group, Ltd., Fairfield, IA.

is superior to the other categories by a wide margin. The low-volatility group had a ratio of .433 versus .330 for the medium-volatility CTAs and .312 for the high-volatility traders.

A similar result was reached when the groups were compared according to the returns divided by the worst drawdowns, although here the margin is not so wide. The ratio for the low-volatility CTAs was 1.86 as compared to 1.61 and 1.46, respectively, for the medium- and high-volatility traders.

The simplest conclusion would be that the race is not always to the swiftest, and that low-volatility CTAs offer the best reward-to-risk trade-offs. However, as with most "simple" conclusions, this may not be wholly accurate. There are several caveats.

First, this study examined groups of CTAs and compared average results. The intelligent investor would certainly want to evaluate each CTA on an individual basis. Second, individual CTA risk profiles tend to shift over time. More important than an absolute comparison may be a consideration of whether a CTA is becoming more or less volatile over time, and to understand why the shift is occurring.

Why? Given a sizeable investment portfolio diversified across a large enough number of high-volatility traders over a long period of time, this strategy may yield the highest total return. An alternative approach to maximizing returns might be to select CTAs offering superior reward-risk profiles—even though they may have lower rates of return—and then leverage those CTAs to achieve the desired return levels. You might consider using notion equity with these CTAs, for example.

The purpose of this exercise is only to provide you with some insights into how to evaluate CTAs. It is up to you to decide how you make use of the results. By this we mean that you might prefer the high-volatility CTAs. If they better meet your investment objectives, you'll at least be able to recognize them and know what you might encounter.

Asymmetrical Risk Evaluation

Before we leave this discussion of volatility, a mention of asymmetrical risk evaluation might interest you. So far we have talked only about volatility as measured by standard deviation. As we learned, it can be either positive or negative. Since it can be on either side of the mean, or average, it is considered symmetrical. The bell-shaped curve graphically depicts the concept.

Exactly how realistic is this? Do investors pour their money into the stock market, for example, without the expectation that it is more likely to make money than lose? What about the so-called "risk-free" bond portfolios? There are some CTAs whose track record includes a history of steady gains, even though they have occasional draw-downs. We are not suggesting that next's month's return could not be in the red. What we are saying is that it may be statistically un-sound to treat a managed futures program that has substantially more positive months than negative as if there is *always* a statistically equal chance that the next month's ROR will be either negative or positive. This flies in the face of experience.

This brings us to the subject of asymmetrical risk evaluation. Two of the leading proponents of this procedure are Brian M. Rom and Kathleen W. Ferguson, principals of Sponsor-Software Systems. They have developed asset-allocation software that utilizes it, and have written an excellent paper on the subject (see Appendix B). Their work treats stocks, bonds, and more traditional types of invest-ments. This discussion attempts to apply their reasoning to managed futures.

Your primary objective, as a potential investor in managed fu-tures, is to forecast the odds that a CTA of your choice will be able to make money for you. To do this, you need to generate the return distributions for each CTA or managed program you are consider-ing. Up to now, we have only discussed it in light of normal and lognormal distribution of returns. Post-Modern Portfolio Theory (PMPT), as used by Mr. Rom and included in his software, uses four-parameter lognormal distribution.

Four-parameter lognormal distribution permits the skewing of the data positively or negatively, depending on whether it is pre-dominantly positive or negative. Skew ratios higher than 1.0 indicate distribution with more returns occurring above the median return, called positive skewness. Ratios below 1.0 represent distributions with more returns below the median, or negative skewness. All the major classes of assets have skewness ratios different than 1.0 because returns are constantly changing. It is improbable to expect returns to come in exactly at the median.

Asymmetrical distribution makes a lot of sense for managed futures programs because of their inherent volatility. Yet advisors who have substantial volatility, but whose returns are mostly positive, should not be penalized. Isn't a lot of upside movement what we all want out of a CTA? The efficient frontier, using standard deviation as the risk measurement, of a CTA with an annual average return of 25 percent and no losing months, but a volatility rating of 10 percent, would not look as attractive as a CTA with a lower return and volatility factor who only made money two-thirds of the time. Which one would you invest with? We'd go with the higher volatility.

Brian Rom expands Post-Modern Portfolio Theory further by redefining the term *risk*. To him, risk is anything below the forecast or target return. His downside risk models focus on calculating the average on the standard deviations of all returns below this target. This moves the reference point higher, from the mean of traditional analysis to the target return level. This is done to be able to quantify the possibility of not reaching the target. Investors using this method get a better insight into the strength of a forecast, where the more traditional approach only deals with the probability of the target being reached. Where one tells you the chances of an occurrence happening, the other spells out the consequences of it not happening. Both are valid and useful insights.

Downside risk analysts use the Sortino ratio, named after Professor Frank Sortino, to rank and/or compare the risk of various asset classes or investment vehicles. It is calculated by dividing the incremental returns over the target by a measure of the downside risk. If the results are positive, the goal has been reached. If negative, it has not been achieved. The size of the numbers indicates the intensity of success or failure.

Unfortunately, at this writing little work has been done with Mr. Rom's software as far as futures traders are concerned. The *Asset Allocation Expert* contains 220 capital asset indexes at the moment. We would like to see the Barclay, MAR, BARRA/MLM, and Norwood Indexes added, along with a database of CTAs, funds, and pools. Mr. Rom's experience is with pension funds, thus the concern with falling short of a target or a pension fund's commitments. Institutional investors will be comfortable with this approach.

EXHIBIT 3.3

Low-Volatility Group
Standard Deviation of Monthly Rate of Return Less Than 5.31%
for the Period 10/1/89 to 9/30/92

Trading Advisors	Compound Annual Return	SD of Monthly ROR	Average Monthly ROR/SD	Worst Draw Down	Average Recovery Time (Mos)	Funds Under Mgmt
1. Trout Trading Company	28.38%	3.58%	0.60	8.88%	4.3	$276M
2. Trinity Money Management, Inc.	23.03%	3.69%	0.49	8.91%	3.0	$12M
3. Luck Trading Co. (Cash Arb)	22.18%	3.45%	0.50	8.59%	3.7	$35M
4. Gandon Fund Mgmt. (Currency)	21.50%	2.88%	0.58	8.00%	4.8	$21M
5. Levin Trading	20.34%	2.50%	0.63	5.46%	2.5	$14M
6. Wessex Fund Management	18.44%	2.85%	0.51	3.86%	2.9	$33M
7. R. Grace & Co., Ltd.	16.98%	3.25%	0.42	7.86%	3.4	$18M
8. Albert L. Hu	16.72%	3.90%	0.35	5.50%	2.3	$24M
9. Telesis Management, Inc.	16.11%	5.07%	0.27	14.07%	5.3	$5M
10. John W. Henry (InterRate)	15.61%	3.85%	0.34	9.70%	6.0	$47M
11. Monaco Asset Management, Inc.	14.90%	3.48%	0.35	11.38%	7.3	$20M
12. Fenchurch Capital Management	14.80%	2.24%	0.53	6.48%	3.2	$124M
13. Hollingsworth Trading Co.	13.60%	5.28%	0.23	10.13%	4.6	$35M
14. Gandon Fund Mgmt. (Global)	13.55%	1.39%	0.77	2.81%	5.0	$40M
15. MAV Partners	12.10%	1.00%	0.96	1.09%	7.0	$87M
16. LaSalle Portfolio Mgmt. (Finan.)	11.22%	3.60%	0.27	12.47%	5.6	$87M
17. Crow Trading, Inc.	9.62%	4.04%	0.21	10.72%	4.7	$11M
18. Sabre Fund Mgmt. (Diversified)	9.01%	3.89%	0.20	15.29%	10.3	$82M
19. Nessler Futures Trading Co.	8.98%	3.59%	0.22	8.70%	5.8	$12M
20. AZF Commodity Mgmt., Inc.	8.88%	3.56%	0.22	10.10%	6.2	$69M

Source: Barclay Trading Group, Ltd., Fairfield, IA.

EXHIBIT 3.4

Medium-Volatility Group
Standard Deviation of Monthly Rate of Return between 5.31% and 8.59% for the Period 10/1/89 to 9/30/92

Trading Advisors	Compound Annual Return	SD of Monthly ROR	Average Monthly ROR/SD	Worst Draw Down	Average Recovery Time (Mos)	Funds Under Mgmt
1. Capital Futures Mgmt. S.N.C.	84.00%	8.37%	0.66	19.48%	4.2	$10M
2. Willowbridge Associates (Argo)	34.62%	8.59%	0.33	21.30%	4.5	$14M
3. Infinity Capital Management Corp.	33.89%	6.96%	0.39	18.38%	4.2	$10M
4. Campbell & Company (Financial)	32.57%	7.20%	0.36	12.11%	3.0	$256M
5. Quest Trading, Inc.	31.69%	5.36%	0.46	10.45%	4.6	$6M
6. Dean Witter Fut. & Curr. (Divers.)	31.36%	8.18%	0.32	17.20%	5.2	$84M
7. Colorado Commodities (Divers.)	30.34%	7.45%	0.34	16.43%	3.7	$7M
8. FX Concepts, Inc.	29.60%	8.39%	0.30	22.99%	4.6	$2,282M
9. Millburn Ridgefield Corp. (Curr)	28.01%	6.16%	0.37	14.94%	6.3	$320M
10. Witter & Lester, Inc.	26.54%	8.41%	0.28	25.69%	4.8	$33M
11. Red Oak Commodity Advisors	24.77%	6.21%	0.33	14.84%	5.2	$52M
12. Chesapeake Capital Corporation	24.39%	7.08%	0.29	16.58%	4.5	$140M
13. Trendview Management, Inc.	24.21%	7.25%	0.29	15.94%	3.8	$52M
14. John W. Henry (Original)	24.14%	8.17%	0.26	19.28%	5.5	$14M
15. Millburn Ridgefield Corp. (Divers)	23.72%	5.72%	0.34	11.22%	5.0	$103M
16. Little Brook Corp. of N.J. (Craft)	22.78%	8.51%	0.24	26.23%	5.0	$40M
17. Range Wise, Inc.	22.58%	7.46%	0.27	28.47%	5.8	$31M
18. Robert M. Tamiso, CTA	22.05%	7.55%	0.26	21.24%	6.0	$7M
19. Pragma, Inc. (Gamma)	21.94%	8.32%	0.24	19.62%	5.0	$18M
20. Lyon Investment Corporation	21.42%	7.39%	0.26	16.38%	3.6	$9M

Source: Barclay Trading Group, Ltd., Fairfield, IA.

EXHIBIT 3.5

High-Volatility Group
Standard Deviation of Monthly Rate of Return Greater Than 8.59% for the Period 10/1/89 to 9/30/92

Trading Advisors	Compound Annual Return	SD of Monthly ROR	Average Monthly ROR/SD	Worst Draw Down	Average Recovery Time (Mos)	Funds Under Mgmt
1. Hawksbill Capital Management	73.71%	22.08%	0.31	61.82%	9.3	$36M
2. Colorado Commodities (Curr./Fin.)	66.97%	9.92%	0.49	17.90%	3.4	$83M
3. Sjo, Inc. (Foreign Financial)	65.48%	11.40%	0.43	14.50%	3.4	$102M
4. Dunn Capital Mgmt. (TOPS)	52.82%	10.72%	0.38	18.16%	6.8	$23M
5. Spackenkill Trading Corp. (Curr.)	46.51%	15.31%	0.28	42.48%	4.0	$8M
6. John W. Henry (Int'l. Forex)	46.30%	10.43%	0.36	24.04%	4.3	$98M
7. Sunrise Commodities (Currency)	46.11%	11.38%	0.34	28.01%	4.5	$117M
8. Abraham Trading Company	42.24%	12.01%	0.30	27.12%	7.5	$26M
9. John W. Henry (Financial/Metals)	40.10%	13.98%	0.27	39.51%	4.6	$528M
10. MRK Enterprises, Inc.	40.04%	11.51%	0.30	34.58%	5.8	$13M
11. Golden Mountain Trading, Inc.	39.10%	10.33%	0.32	26.63%	7.0	$46M
12. FX 500, LTD.	37.16%	9.58%	0.32	7.22%	3.3	$64M
13. John W. Henry (KT Global)	34.29%	11.25%	0.28	29.12%	7.5	$21M
14. Waldner Financial Corporation	33.37%	11.13%	0.28	29.11%	3.9	$22M
15. EMC Capital Management	31.96%	15.28%	0.22	34.85%	7.0	$89M
16. Rabar Market Research	30.00%	9.29%	0.28	26.79%	9.3	$63M
17. Winchester Asset Management	29.37%	8.75%	0.29	16.42%	4.3	$13M
18. CCA Capital Management (Forex)	28.30%	11.50%	0.24	32.38%	4.1	$41M
19. Gaiacorp Ireland Limited	27.64%	14.60%	0.21	46.12%	14.0	$85M
20. Mark J. Walsh & Company	26.76%	13.20%	0.21	27.40%	6.0	$37M

Source: Barclay Trading Group, Ltd., Fairfield, IA.

4

Understanding the Nature of the Risk of Loss in the Futures Markets

The discussion of volatility included one serious caveat, i.e., standard deviation ignores the direction of the data being measured. A CTA could have a very low volatility rating and bleed to death. Another CTA could be a member of the "Wild Bunch," yet have a track record George Soros would envy.

As one who is considering an investment in managed futures, the direction of the monthly rate of return—whether it is up or down—is of the utmost importance. For this reason, we need to talk a little about the risk of loss of equity and how professional traders deal with it.

First of all, every commodity trader loses money in the futures market on a regular basis. If you're not prepared to face this reality, there's no point in reading any further. You've got your money's worth from this book.

Entering successful trades on a regular basis doesn't distinguish a successful trader from a born loser. Money management does! Survivability does! "Cut your losses short; let your winners run!" The greater the loss, the harder it is to recover. That's what the Loss Recovery Table below demonstrates.

Loss Recovery Table

% Loss	% Needed for Breakeven
5	5.26
20	25.00
30	42.86
40	66.67
50	100.00
70	233.33
90	900.00
100	Impossible

If your advisor loses 50 percent in month one and earns 50 percent in month two, are you even? No! You still have a 25 percent drawdown of equity based on what you started with at the beginning of month one.

Futures trading is usually a very fast-moving, in-and-out type of investment, compared to most others. It is a rare trader, called a position trader, who holds trades over a few weeks. Most trades last a few days at most, many are offset the same day they are opened. This is called day trading.

Futures traders are like fly-fishermen. They constantly cast their bait (equity) into the stream of price activity flowing through the futures exchanges. Sometimes they'll use a market order, which generally assures them a bite. Once the order is filled, they check to see if it is of legal limit (profitable). If not, they quickly toss it back. Other times they use a fly (order) with one or more feathers or other limitations (stop order, market-if-touched, on close or open) attached. Sometimes these are hit, sometimes not. If the order is filled, the CTA checks to see if it is worth taking home for dinner. Occasionally, your angler ties into a trophy-size trout. An average distribution of the catch for a successful CTA might break out like this:

Breakout of Trades

Total Trades	100
Winners	50
Losers	50

Breakdown of Winners

Small	40
Medium	8
Large	2

Breakdown of Losers

Small	39
Medium	10
Large	1

The art of making money in the futures market revolves around the concept of capital preservation. In the book *Market Wizards* by Jack Schwager, Paul Tudor Jones, a legendary futures trader, says, "The most important rule of trading is to play a great defense, not a great offense." If you can stay in the markets with enough of your equity intact, you'll eventually bring home a record catch. And, you'll have plenty of dinner size fish as well.

With this concept in mind, you need to prepare a list of questions to ask prospective trading advisors. Here are a few suggestions:

1. What has been your largest monthly drawdown of equity in dollars and percent of money under management?

2. How long did your largest losing streak last?

3. In a single day, what was the most you ever lost?

4. How often do you go on losing binges?

5. Once you experience a major setback, how long does it take to reverse?

6. What steps, psychological and/or tactical, do you take to expedite a recovery?

7. What is your overall philosophy regarding losing other people's money?

8. Do you have a written list of money management rules?

9. What changes or modifications do you make to your trading systems when you're in a drawdown?

10. How do you adjust your trading system to changing market conditions, particularly major increases in volatility?

11. What would prompt you to completely halt trading (stand aside the market) and how would you know when to reenter?

12. Do you trade with stop loss orders and what are your trading principles regarding stops?

13. Explain your concept, pro or con, of diversification.

14. Do you calculate risk-to-reward ratios before putting on a trade?

15. Tell me what the worst case scenario would be if I invested in your program.

A frank discussion of risk often separates the rank amateurs from the consummate professionals. From talking with hundreds of professional traders, brokers, and CTAs, we know that the good ones do not avoid or shy away from the subject. All of them have had, and have survived, major drawdowns. This is the nature of high risk–high reward investment. A refusal or avoidance of the subject on the part of a CTA could be considered as a denial and you might use this attitude as a Macro-Disqualifier.

We've also found that these traders have a certain detachment from winning and losing. It is an impersonal market that gives and takes away money. The CTA who takes the process to heart cannot survive long. Therefore, look for this impersonal attitude.

You also want to invest with someone who has done some serious thinking on the subject—who has had a serious run of ill luck and snapped right back. We'd be more uncomfortable with a trader who has never taken a serious loss because you have no way of gauging how he or she will deal with it when it comes. Or, you may have the feeling that person isn't being wholly forthright.

Documentation is reassuring. This can be a written list of trading rules. For example, the CTA may risk only 10 percent of a client's total equity on any one position, or halt trading in an account for evaluation after sustaining a 25 percent drawdown, or quit day trading a particular market after three consecutive losses. The CTA may take a short vacation from the market entirely following five straight losing trades in any one market.

The exact rules are not as important as knowing the trader has carefully thought out how best he or she can preserve your equity. If enough of the initial capital is kept intact, sooner or later a competent trading advisor will generate some very successful trades. It is not uncommon for a very small percentage, say less than 5 percent, of the total trades to generate 80 percent or 90 percent of the profits.

Novice investors often ask traders why they don't get out of the market during drawdowns. The answer goes back to the discussion about the randomness of all markets and the fact that we are trying to anticipate what will happen at some time in the future. No one knows for sure when a market will trend up or down for an extended period of time. But we do know it will happen!

The phenomenon is not unique to the futures market. Take the Dow as an example. The University of Michigan did a study of the bull market in stocks between 1982 and 1987. It lasted 1275 days. An investor who was in the market every day would have made 26.3 percent. But if that same investor was out of the market on the 10 biggest days, he or she would have made only 18.3 percent. Miss the 20 biggest days and you give up another 5 percent. Missing the top 30 drops you to an 8.5 percent return. Stand aside the 40 best days and you are looking at a return of 4.3 percent. In other words, missing just the best 3 percent of the trading days reduced an investor's return by over 80 percent.

Here's an example from the records of a well-known CTA, but from a slightly different perspective. This advisor had a drawdown that lasted approximately six months. It required nine months to reach the peak high that immediately preceded the drawdown period. If an investor missed the first month of the recovery, that person would have had to wait 12 months to restore the lost equity. Missing one month added three to the recovery period. Or, if that same investor waited two months to get back in, it would have taken 17 months to get whole.

The lessons are simple. First, drawdowns are going to occur. Second, you never will know exactly when the big winners will strike. These two facts of futures trading are exaggerated by the great amount of leverage possible.

The futures trader deposits a small amount of margin money for each contract to be traded. This represents only enough to show good faith. Here are a few examples:

Contract	Size	Value	Extension	Initial Margin	%
Corn	5000 bu.	$2.50/bu.	$12,500.00	$270.00	2%
KR-CRB Index	500 × KR-CRB Index	220	$110,000.00	$1,500.00	1%
Gold	100 troy oz.	$400/oz.	$40,000.00	$700.00	6%
Sugar	112,000 lbs.	10¢/lb.	$11,200.00	$700.00	6%
T-Bonds	$50,000	100%	$50,000.00	$1,000.00	2%

The margin is usually less than 5 percent of the value of the contract. That's a 20:1 leveraging factor. Let's use gold as an example. If it moves $5.00 per ounce, you would gain or lose 30 percent based on the $1,500.00 margin. Moves of this magnitude can occur daily. In three days of this kind of activity, you could go down or up 100 percent.

It is this tremendous amount of leveraging that makes futures trading so speculative. The BARRA/MLM Index, as you may remember, was unleveraged to tame the speculative nature of the beast and reveal the economic value of the futures markets.

As you search for an advisor, ask about how they manage the leverage. For example, some CTAs will only commit half of an investment to the market at any one time. Or they may shut down trading after a prearranged amount, say 25 percent to 50 percent, of the initial equity is lost.

Remember what Paul Tudor Jones said, "Trade defensively!" Think about surviving until the mother lode is hit. Run away from losses so you can trade another day. Our experience indicates that putting the laws of probability to work for you gives you an edge— an edge that can help you protect your investment on the downside and improve your chances for success on the upside.

5

Quantifying the Risk and Reward of Managed Futures Programs

Ask five football fans which statistic is the best indicator of a great quarterback, and you'll probably get five different answers—the touchdown to interception ratio, pass completion percentage, consecutive games played, release time, or win/loss record. While this debate might make for interesting half-time talk, obviously no one statistic is adequate to encompass all of the important characteristics of an athlete's past performance.

The analysis of money manager performance is very similar. First and most obvious, no single statistic tells a complete story about a CTA's past performance. For example, rate of return tells us nothing about a trader's volatility, while worst drawdown says nothing about upside performance. Taken together, however, these two begin to paint an interesting picture—they show us the relationship between the historical reward and risk of the CTA's performance. In fact, these two measures combined are the basis of the Sterling Ratio developed by Deane Sterling Jones.

The Sterling Ratio (SR) compares a trader's average rate of return (ROR) over three consecutive years to that trader's average largest drawdown in equity during the same period plus 10 percent.

$$SR = \frac{\text{3--yr Avg. ROR}}{\text{Average of the largest drawdowns} + 10\%}$$

This ratio attempts to resolve the risk-reward dichotomy. Or to put it another way, you deserve more reward when you assume more risk. The 10 percent tacked on to the drawdown is to adjust for the fact that shorter-term calculations of drawdown are understated compared to the annual drawdown figure.

Let's look at an example. CTA Alpha has an average annual rate of return of 35 percent and the average of his largest drawdowns for the same three-year period comes to 20 percent. CTA Beta has an average return of 25 percent and losses averaging 15 percent.

Alpha	Beta
$\frac{35}{20+10} = 1.16$	$\frac{25}{15+10} = 1$

The Sterling Ratio for Alpha is 1.16; Beta's is 1. With this ratio, the higher the better. Therefore, we'll supposedly get more bang for our buck with the first CTA. The relationship between Alpha's gains and Alpha's losses is more favorable.

It also makes sense to look at the track record of each CTA to see when losses occurred. If, for example, one of the CTAs was on a four-month losing streak that extended over more than one year—November, December, January, February—the drawdown for one of the years would include only November and December, since the calculation is based on a calendar year.

We also like to take a look at the volatility of the drawdowns. Violent ups and downs are more disconcerting than mild ones. Let's say two CTAs have an average drawdown of 20 percent over three years, but one track record shows figures of 5 percent, 50 percent, and 5 percent and the other is 20 percent, 20 percent, and 20 percent. Or, it could be that one CTA has drawdowns of 5 percent, 25 percent, and 30 percent compared to 30 percent, 25 percent, and 5 percent. If the ROR were the same, all of these CTAs would have the same Sterling Ratio. You would then have to ask yourself if you can deal with the possibility of your advisor taking another 50 percent hit, as the first CTA did. Looking at the second pair of CTAs, one has drawdowns that are accelerating, while the other is decelerating. Which one are you more comfortable with?

It is for reasons like the above that we stated at the beginning of this chapter that you must examine more than one statistical study in your analysis. This leads us to another ratio that is commonly used to evaluate alternative CTAs, and even alternative asset classes. It is the Sharpe Ratio.

This ratio attempts to extract from a CTA's monthly or annual ROI the portion that can be attributed solely to risk associated with the CTA's trading. Again, the assumption is that the higher the risk, the higher the returns should be to justify assuming the risk. It accomplishes this by subtracting the rate of return that could be earned if the trading equity was invested in a totally risk-free investment, such as three-month U.S. Treasury bills. The remainder equals the amount of return that rewards the risk taking. It is divided by the standard deviation of the monthly or annual rate of return.

For example, let's say a CTA has an annual return of 25 percent. From that we subtract the risk-free rate of say 5 percent, giving us 20 percent. This figure would be divided by the CTA's standard deviation of his or her monthly returns. For this example, we'll use a CTA in the Medium-Volatility Group with SD of 7.75. The Sharpe Ratio would be 2.58.

A minor variation of the Sharpe Ratio is the Efficiency Index. The only difference is you do not subtract the risk-free rate of return from the annual rate of return before dividing by the standard deviation. In our example, you would divide 25 by 7.75 for an Efficient Index of 3.2. Some analysts believe this is a more accurate tool, especially when comparing fixed-income instruments with more speculative types of asset classes, like futures or managed futures.

As we've mentioned often, drawdowns of equity are critical. You can't trade without the margin money. For this reason, financial analysts have developed various ways of studying drawdowns.

Probably the most common and easiest is simply comparing one CTA's worst drawdown with others. Most analysts express it as a percentage of equity, rather than absolute dollars. Sometimes you may look at just the worst drawdown in any month, quarter, or year. We prefer to calculate the worst cumulative drawdown, no matter how long it lasts. This way you might be comparing one CTA's drawdown over one or two months with another's that lasted six months or longer.

We look at it this way because drawdowns affect a trader's confidence, as well as his or her ability to recover. The longer a drawdown lasts, the more likely investors will withdraw their money. This is a double whammy for the trader. Additionally, it makes raising new money more difficult. So now you have a trader losing confidence, deserted by his investors, and a demoralized sales force. As if that weren't enough, the trader is also getting bad press in *Futures Magazine*. All because of a few losing months.

Another way of viewing the return on investment is comparing the number of winning months to the number of losing ones. Over time, this is a measure of consistency. The higher the percentage, the more consistent the winnings should be. The theory is, all things being equal, a trader who has twice as many winning months as losing months should be more successful.

As you probably guessed by now, this theory has its exceptions. There are traders who cut their winning trades short and let their losers run. Once they get a little profit in a position, they panic—offsetting the position prematurely. When a trade goes in the red, they don't have the confidence or experience to stop the bleeding. You can root out these unfortunate souls by matching their track record with their rate of winning months to losing months. This would be another Macro-Disqualifier.

There are a couple of other ratios you may want to consult from time to time. For example, Jack Schwager proposed the Gain-to-Retracement Ratio (GRR), as described in Morton S. Baratz's classic book on managed futures, *The Investor's Guide to Futures Money Management*. This ratio compares the annualized compounded rate of return to the Average Maximal Retracement (AMR). AMR is defined as the largest average decline in the account's equity since inception. This means it is measuring actual loss of initial equity, rather than profits that may have been earned. Thus it is closest to what many investors think of when they begin to think about the loss they may sustain.

Barclay Trading Group has its own ratio, as do many MOMs (Managers of Managers). The Barclay Ratio (BR) equals the VAMI (Valued Added Monthly Index) divided by the standard deviation of the monthly returns. Although similar in certain aspects to the Sharpe Ratio, it is a much higher correlation with percentage of profitability over 12-month time windows than other ratios. The VAMI is explained in more detail later in this chapter when we discuss the track record, since it is a part of it.

Time windows are another way of analyzing CTAs. Think of them as moving averages of various lengths. You take what you believe to be the most useful or meaningful statistics and isolate them over various time intervals. You could use monthly, quarterly, semi-annually, nine-month, or annual periods, or all of the above. Worst drawdown, highest rate of return, or standard deviation are good examples. You ask the questions:

- What is this CTA's worst drawdown of any given three-month period of time?
- What is this CTA's highest rate of return over that same time period?
- What was his or her standard deviation (volatility) over this time window?

Each time window is calculated by rolling one month's statistic forward and dropping the last month's off, then recalculating.

A year breaks out like this:

Time Windows	3-Month	6-Month	9-Month	12-Month
1				
2				
3	1			
4	2			
5	3			
6	4	1		
7	5	2		
8	6	3		
9	7	4	1	
10	8	5	2	
11	9	6	3	
12	10	7	4	1

You would have 10 quarterly time window figures; seven semiannual; four nine-month; and a single annual. Having this data helps you answer questions like:

- Should I stay with this CTA for another three months?
- Over any given six-month time window, what would be the worst I should expect?
- Over what time window in the past had this CTA been most productive?

Now, we've come to the question of how to analyze the overall track record of a CTA or, what do we really mean when we use the term "track record"? Usually, we are referring to the table(s) recording all the activity that has occurred in accounts managed by a registered CTA and published in his or her disclosure document. It is the equivalent of a prospectus, which would be required for a new stock issue or a placement document used to inform investors about a limited partnership.

CTA disclosure documents are regulated by the Commodity Futures Trading Commission (CFTC). They provide prospective investors with much of the information needed to decide if they want to invest with a specific CTA. Besides the track record, there is plenty of legalese describing the risk involved in futures trading. It also provides descriptions of the CTA's trading system, a biographical sketch of the principals, and an explanation of all the costs involved (management fees, incentive fees, commissions, etc.).

Most of the legal jargon is boilerplate. You need to remember, as you read it, who paid to have it prepared. Therefore, you can assume it primarily protects the CTA. When the CFTC reviews any disclosure document, it does so only from the standpoint of the appropriate regulations. The CFTC does not even consider whether the trading system described or the CTA has a good chance of making you money. That is not their province. It is yours! If a CTA or someone selling a program told you the CFTC approved their trading approach and/or recommend the program, this would be a Macro-Disqualifier.

The CFTC, with the help of the National Futures Association, regulates CTAs. Compliance audits are regularly conducted. Part of a routine audit involves testing track records used in disclosure documents. This includes everything from simple math checks to requesting to see all the documentation on select accounts. If a track record indicated, for example, that a CTA made or lost money trading French francs on a certain day, the auditors might ask to see the order tickets, daily run (record of each trade executed on a certain day), customer statements, and proof the French franc traded at that price on that day. Historical charts are usually used to verify trading ranges.

Before we get too far with this discussion of disclosure documents, we need to remind you of what we said earlier. Not everyone who can take discretion in your trading account is required to provide a disclosure document. Remember, your spouse's favorite nephew and your futures broker, doing it at your request and for your convenience, are generally exempt. Also exempt are CTAs who do not hold themselves out to the public as CTAs and who handle small amounts of money and a few accounts in a year's time. In other words, not every person who wants to trade for you has to provide you with a disclosure document.

To find out who does or doesn't, simply ask any prospective advisor for one. If they don't have one, ask why. If you are not sure their answer is in compliance with federal regulations, you can call the NFA Information Center and discuss the situation. While on the line, inquire about the status of their registration, how long they have been in business, and if they have any past or pending customer complaints.

The heart and soul of a disclosure document is the track record. CFTC regulations require that CTAs include in their track records all accounts they have had discretion over for the past three years. "Dis-docs," as they are known within the industry, have a six-month shelf life. On the cover page is a printed date on which the dis-doc expires. This is to make sure investors get a reasonably updated picture of the trader's performance before investing. Regulators want to discourage CTAs who have a serious losing streak from hiding this fact from potential patrons.

Occasionally, you may be given an expired dis-doc for preview. This is within regulations, but you must be given a current one prior to investing. Track records are usually updated monthly. If the dis-doc you have been given is three, four, or five months old, ask for an update to the track record. You want to be as current as possible.

Now, let's specifically talk about track records. First, look to see if it is a real or hypothetical track record. CFTC regulation 4.41(b)(1) requires that all track records be clearly marked HYPOTHETICAL if that is what they are. Additionally, they must have the following paragraph clearly displayed:

HYPOTHETICAL OR SIMULATED PERFORMANCE RESULTS HAVE CER-TAIN INHERENT LIMITATIONS. UNLIKE AN ACTUAL PERFORMANCE RECORD, SIMULATED RESULTS DO NOT REPRESENT ACTUAL TRAD-ING. ALSO, SINCE THE TRADES HAVE NOT ACTUALLY BEEN EXE-CUTED, THE RESULTS MAY HAVE UNDER- OR OVERCOMPENSATED FOR THE IMPACT, IF ANY, OF CERTAIN MARKET FACTORS, SUCH AS LACK OF LIQUIDITY. SIMULATED TRADING PROGRAMS IN GENERAL ARE ALSO SUBJECT TO THE FACT THAT THEY ARE DESIGNED WITH THE BENEFIT OF HINDSIGHT. NO REPRESENTATION IS BEING MADE THAT ANY ACCOUNT WILL OR IS LIKELY TO ACHIEVE PROFITS OR LOSSES SIMILAR TO THOSE SHOWN.

Consider hypothetical track records generally as a Macro-Disqualifier. Here are some of the reasons:

1. Hypothetical trading is to real-life trading as playing a computer-simulated golf game by yourself is to playing a $5.00 Nassau against your club pro. The emotional pitch that comes from losing hard-earned money is missing. The pressure and stress are absent. You don't make the same mistakes in practice as you do in the game.

2. It's too easy to deliberately, or even unknowingly, fudge the results. Some hypothetical track records we've seen have neglected to include commissions. Others were rigged to get the best possible fill on every order. Still others somehow traded on limit up or limit down days and even on days the exchanges were closed.

3. Hypothetical results are often computer-generated. A sharp operator can run the program in dozens of different markets, until one friendly to the system is found. Or they can fine-tune the trading system to perform well with a knowledge of historical markets.

You should only partially rely on actual past performance and never on hypothetical results. Later on we'll quantify what we mean by "partially rely" on past performance. The CFTC requires the following statement to accompany all track records: "Past performance is not indicative of future results."

The CFTC also specifies the structure of track records. Modifications are made from time to time, but the standard one contains nine columns—Month/Year, Beginning Net Asset Value (BNAV), Additions, Withdrawals, Net Performance, Ending Net Asset Value (ENAV), Rate of Return (ROR), VAMI, and Annual Rate of Return. There are only two areas that cause any confusion: the Additions/Withdrawals and the VAMI.

Moving left to right, the first column specifies the month and year. The second is the BNAV and represents the actual funds in the account at the beginning of the month. Additions, column three, details equity that was added that month, while the next column shows what was taken out. Net performance, in the fifth place, contains the results for the month, which includes both realized gains and losses from closed positions and unrealized gains and losses from open positions less deductions for various charges, such as exchange fees, commissions, incentive fees, and others. Ending Net Asset Value equals BNAV plus or minus Additions/Withdrawals and the Net Performance for the month. The Monthly Rate of Return is found by dividing Net Performance by BNAV.

At this point, we encounter the first area of confusion. Several questions arise. If a large amount of money is withdrawn from the account right after the beginning of the month, the CTA did not have that money available to trade that month. Or, if a large amount was added, the CTA had it available to trade, but it's not included in the BNAV. Either of these situations distort the ROR figure. With some very large CTAs with a lot of activity or CTAs with a small amount of trading equity, this can create material problems.

To compensate, the CFTC requires CTAs to footnote how they handle additions and withdrawals. Some have created daily balances and calculated ROR each day, much like a bank handles your interest-bearing checking account. Other CTAs set rules that exclude accounts that have major (10 percent or more) additions or withdrawals in the given month. You need to read the footnotes that accompany the tables to understand how all this is handled.

The next to the last column is the VAMI (Value Added Monthly Index). The CFTC requires the VAMI figure so that investors can easily compare one program with another. It represents the gain or loss of $1,000 invested in the trading program at the beginning of each year.

Think of it as an index. At day one of each year, it is set at $1,000. At the end of each month, the $1,000 is multiplied by 1 plus the rate of return. If the rate of return is positive, the $1,000 increases. If negative, it decreases. At the end of the next month, the amount of the VAMI is again multiplied by 1 plus the ROR. This continues throughout the year. Here's a six-month example:

Month	Rate of Return	VAMI
		$1,000.00
1	+5%	$1,050.00
2	−10%	$945.00
3	+5%	$992.25
4	+5%	$1,041.86
5	+3%	$1,073.12
6	−6%	$1,008.73

The final column of the track record is the Annual Rate of Return for the calendar year.

In some dis-docs, you may find more than one track record. This is done to showcase a particular program a CTA offers. These are referred to as extracted tables, since they are taken from composite tables. For example, a CTA may have one program that trades only the agricultural commodities or foreign currencies. He or she may be particularly proud of his or her specialized program. Or, the CTA may have corrected what he or she thinks was a serious flaw in his or her trading system. One track record shows the overall results, while another indicates what happened after the bug was removed. In other words, you need to carefully study what you are looking at and READ ALL THE FOOTNOTES.

Always be aware that the figures are composites of all the CTA's accounts. The annual results might be very attractive, but this does not mean every individual account made that much money. Some investors could very well have lost. They might have prematurely withdrawn from the program or their account was traded in some markets that were unfriendly to the CTA's system. A 30 percent annual return doesn't mean that was what you would have received if you had invested with this particular CTA.

6

Analyzing the Risk and Reward of Managed Futures Programs

As we did in Chapter 3 with volatility, you can use any statistic you generate or collect as a filter. We, for example, ran the volatility data through three different-sized filters—categorizing the CTAs' volatility into ranges—high, medium, or low.

A simpler approach is to rank the data from highest to lowest or lowest to highest. Data covering percentage of months profitable might be ranked highest to lowest, while drawdown of volatility data could be lowest to highest. This approach attempts to place what is usually considered positive (high return and/or low volatility/drawdown) at the top of the lists. The art in this process is to choose the specific data that provides a dependable insight into how the CTA will perform in the future.

You'll also want to compare rates of return of your trader to the BARRA/MLM Index. The difference between this index and your trader's returns quantifies his or her skills. The bigger the difference, providing it is positive, the greater his or her trading expertise. But just like when comparing stocks analysts to the Dow, there will be periods when the index does better. In the long run—i.e., over a period of years—your advisor should generate a profit in excess of the "insurance premium" paid by the hedgers to speculators for assuming the risk of price movement.

Once you grade all the CTA candidates you're considering by all the statistical characteristics you consider important, you'll begin to uncover patterns. A CTA who ranks in the top five of all the categories may be worth more investigation. Or you might be warned off a CTA you are seriously considering because he or she turned up as being more volatile than you were prepared for.

Another analytical approach is to assign values to each category. A first place in each statistical ranking gets five points; second place, four; third, three; fourth, two; fifth, one. Once all the points are assigned and accumulated, you rank your CTAs by their totals. Then you continue your investigation from the top of the list.

Serious investors can create a spreadsheet of CTAs on their personal computers. You feed the basic data on each candidate into it and the machine does the ranking. This becomes particularly handy if you're constantly on the lookout for new talent.

You'll also want to compare your trader(s) against his or her peers. There are three indexes to consider. First, there is the MAR Index, or *Managed Account Report* Index. It was designed to be representative of what a professional CTA would accomplish.

During January of each year, the MAR staff selects 25 prominent CTAs trading $30 million or more as a sampling of the entire universe of professional CTAs. The index is dollar-weighted. MAR also generates indexes of managed pools and funds, which you can use for comparison of these types of programs (see Exhibit 6.1).

The second one to become familiar with is the Barclay CTA Index. Where the MAR Index was meant to be representative, the Barclay Index was designed to be comprehensive, or at least more comprehensive. Its design parameters are:

- *Weighting:* Equal weight is given to each CTA included in the index. The index is not dollar-weighted.
- *Inclusion factors:* The only criterion for inclusion in the Barclay Index is that a CTA must have had at least four years of actual performance history prior to inclusion. A CTA's per-

EXHIBIT 6.1

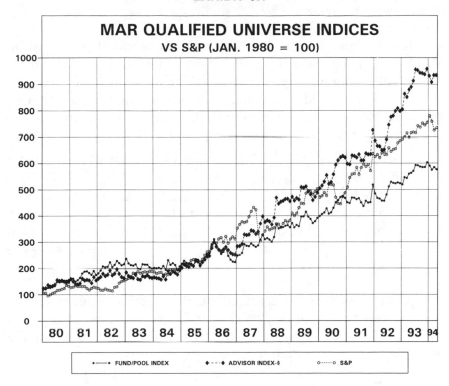

Source: *Managed Accounts Reports*, New York, NY

formance is included beginning with the start of his or her fifth year of actual trading. The only exception to this rule is that if an established CTA introduces new investment programs, the subsequent programs are included from the beginning of their third year of trading.

The inclusion policy of the Barclay Index may make it more democratic, but it also causes some problems with continuity. For example, in 1980, it included 16 CTAs. Now it has over 250. The problem of continuity is common to all indexes, even the Dow. In 1896, the Dow was composed of 12 stocks. It then increased to 20 in

1916 and 30 by 1928. Only 12 of the original 30 stocks are still in the index, given a number of name changes. And, over the past 50 years, there have been 16 substitutions.

Like the Dow, the Barclay CTA Index is subdivided into multiple subindices, seven to be exact. The Barclay subindices facilitate comparisons among seven subsets of managed programs. Five of these subsets are based on portfolio composition and two on trading style. In order for a managed program to be included in any of these subindices, it must meet the following criteria:

1. The program must have at least 12 months prior performance history.

2. Extracted performance is NOT acceptable. In other words, the program must be set up from the start to trade a certain group of commodities. A CTA cannot analyze her overall trading activity and decide to create a subgroup because she has done well in, say, the currencies.

For purposes of index construction, the first full calendar year of performance and any prior partial year of performance is excluded. The reason for this one-year exclusion is an attempt to avoid the upward bias of the selection process.

Subindices

Based on Portfolio Criteria

1. *Barclay Agricultural Traders Index:* An equal-weighted composite of managed programs that trade agricultural markets, e.g., grains, meats, foods. In 1994, there were 16 agricultural programs included in the index.

2. *Barclay Currency Traders Index:* An equal-weighted composite of managed programs that trade currency futures and/or cash forwards in the interbank market. In 1994, there were 59 currency programs included in the index.

3. *Barclay Diversified Traders Index:* An equal-weighted composite of managed programs that trade a diversified portfolio.

In 1994, there were 170 diversified programs included in the index.

4. *Barclay Energy Traders Index:* An equal-weighted composite of managed programs that trade energy markets. In 1994, there were 15 energy programs included in the index.

5. *Barclay Financials and Metals Traders Index:* An equal-weighted composite of managed programs that trade primarily financial or financial and metals. In 1994, there were 89 financial and metals programs included in the index.

Based on Trading Style

6. *Barclay Discretionary Traders Index:* An equal-weighted composite of managed programs whose approach is at least 75 percent discretionary or judgmental. In 1994, there were 92 discretionary programs included in the index.

7. *Barclay Systematic Traders Index:* An equal-weighted composite of managed programs whose approach is at least 95 percent systematic. In 1994, there were 202 systematic programs included in the index. (See Exhibit 6.2.)

By being able to compare your CTAs or prospective candidates with a subindex that more closely resembles what or how they trade, you often get a more accurate picture of how they are doing. This is particularly true over shorter periods of time, like a year or less. The reason is that specific markets can be friendly at one point in time, while another group is hostile to profit taking. Or one group may be full of opportunities, while another is flat. One may be trending smoothly for long periods of time, making it "easy" to trade; a second may be lurching up and down without any apparent rhyme or rationale.

The Norwood Index

The third index, the Norwood Index, measures commodity-trading funds and takes a somewhat different approach to measuring suc-

EXHIBIT 6.2

Compound Annual Returns
1987–1993

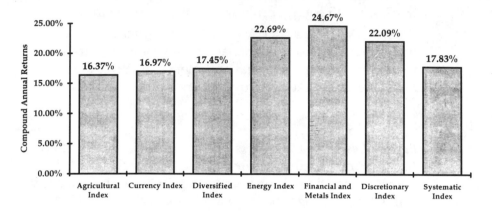

Source: Barclay Trading Group, Ltd., Fairfield, IA.

cess. Dan Stark, president of Stark Research and owner of the Norwood Index, makes a distinction between returns based on VAMIs and those based on NAVs. It is his position that the problem of additions and withdrawals, as we discussed in Chapter 5, distorts VAMI-based indexes. For this reason, he uses net asset value.

The Norwood Index was first published in 1978, when it began tracking nine commodity funds. As of this printing, there are 188 funds worldwide included in the index. (See Exhibit 6.3.) Note that traditional technical and cyclical analysis are used to forecast the index's highs, lows, and trading range.

It is assembled monthly by collecting each fund's ending net asset value from the fund sponsor or general partner. Percentage changes from the previous month's ending NAV per unit are then evaluated. The Norwood's simple average performance is calculated by summing each fund's monthly percentage change and dividing by the total number of funds in the index for that month. Year-to-date performance for the index is determined by compounding

EXHIBIT 6.3

Norwood Index

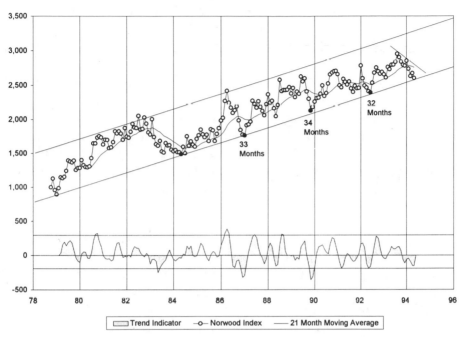

monthly returns in a hypothetical $1,000 investment and measuring the percent change of this investment throughout the year. If you are considering a fund at some point, this index makes a good reference. MAR also publishes a fund index.

Before we leave the subject of indexes, you need to become aware of the concept and impact of survivorship. All indexes are modified by this phenomenon. It simply means that the better stocks, stock traders, CTAs, or whatever is being indexed, stay in existence and on their index. The Dow performs well because the stocks included in it withstood the test of time. The fittest survive.

This law of nature prevails for CTAs as well as amoebas. The selection criterion for the MAR Index was for "prominent" CTAs with over $30 million under management. It takes time and success to become prominent and raise that much money. To make it to the Barclay Index, a four-year track record is required. To continually trade futures for four years requires skill, experience, and a certain amount of success. Therefore, both of these indexes are biased in favor of the more accomplished. Keep this in mind when you do comparisons.

Your comparisons become more reliable, the more variables you remove from the equation. Think of all the sundry things that affect performance. Take trading style as an example. We classify traders as discretionary or systematic. The former weigh all the information available and make a decision. The latter create a system and follow its signals religiously. Generally speaking, discretionary futures traders do better in choppy, sideways markets; systematic traders prefer trending markets.

This implies that the type of market—whether it's trending or not—would be another key, which it is. You must compare traders over the same markets and the same periods of time. It would be unfair to judge a corn trader from 1965 to 1970 to a deutsche mark trader from 1985 to 1988. The corn trader just didn't have the opportunities that the D-mark trader did, since corn traded for over five years in a narrow price range. The D-mark, on the other hand, doubled in value over the three years in question—steadily increasing each year without a serious retracement. All a CTA had to do was to stay long and move protective stops higher once a week.

As you evaluate a CTA during flat market conditions, which may be defined as very narrow trading ranges, it is important to evaluate his or her reaction. Does the trader migrate to greener pastures? Does he or she have the experience and knowledge to trade corn and currencies at the same time? Can the trading system adapt? You are looking for patience and discipline. As Kenny Rogers would say, there's a time to stand pat and a time to fold. Experienced traders wait for opportunities; gamblers force their hand. Learn to distinguish between the two.

7

Using Statistics to Analyze CTAs

So far, we have provided an insight into some of the statistics you might want to collect to evaluate the performance of CTAs. Now we're going to share with you one approach to analysis of the data.

As we work through this example, you'll notice that our CTA selection process is as much subjective as it is objective. If CTA selection could be reduced to a totally objective methodology, we'd computerize it and every investor would want the same CTA. That person would manage all the money in the industry. In Chapter 2, we saw that there are several ways of creating a CTA performance baseline. The selection process works in the same way. We'll walk you through our thinking to provide you with a foundation on which to build your own.

Rule number one is that the reward expected from a trading advisor is matched by the risk (see Exhibit 7.1). No pain, no gain. Meager risk, meager reward.

To quantify the risk-reward dichotomy, we like to run a series of Efficient Frontiers (see Exhibit 7.2). This is a concept from Modern Portfolio Theory. You begin with your current investment portfolio and run a baseline analysis. This tells you where you stand before

EXHIBIT 7.1

Risk vs. Reward

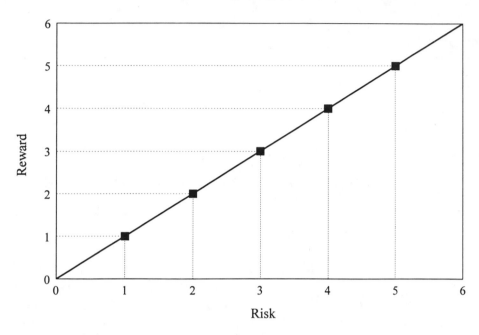

Source: Securities Corporation of America, Cedar Rapids, IA.

making a commitment to a managed futures program. Then you add managed futures proxy data to your asset-allocation mix. You can use one or more of the CTA indexes previously described. The Barclay CTA Index was specifically designed to emulate a portfolio of CTAs. Or, you might input the MAR Index, which is comprised of leading CTAs. There are also the Norwood and the BARRA/MLM Indexes, the latter being one of the more conservative, since it is unleveraged. Choose the one you think might most closely resemble the type of CTA you'd select.

In this step, you start adjusting your "new" portfolio with the addition of 5 percent, 10 percent, and 15 percent managed futures. You deduct the amount to be invested in managed futures from the

EXHIBIT 7.2

Efficient Frontier

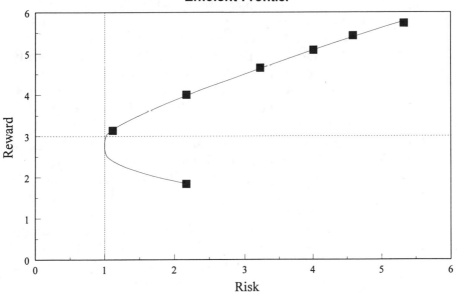

Objective is to locate the point where you get the greatest amount of reward with the least amount of risk (coordinates 3:1).

Source: Securities Corporation of Iowa, Cedar Rapids, IA.

asset class you'll be converting to managed futures. You study the Efficient Frontier graphs of the various asset allocations to determine the best mix. Which allocation gives you the most reward for the least risk? It usually comes out indicating 10 to 15 percent should be in managed futures.

You now know approximately how much you can invest in managed futures. For example, if the most efficient percentage in managed futures is 10 percent and your total portfolio is worth $500,000, you should consider investing $50,000. This is very important because it defines which and/or how many CTAs you can select. Most CTAs have a minimum investment requirement, which can range between $5,000 and $1 million or more. Additionally, there are some tremendous advantages in being able to invest in multiple CTAs, as we'll see in a later chapter.

Now that you know you can invest $50,000, your broker or advisor can generate a list of CTAs or pools with minimums of $50,000 or less. The reason CTAs have minimums for individual accounts is twofold. First, most professional CTAs have a carefully defined trading system, which includes diversification into several markets. To make the CTA's approach work, the investor must have enough equity to trade all the commodities and/or markets called for by the system.

The second reason is staying power. Enough money should be invested to withstand a drawdown, which may occur in month one. Probably the biggest reason investors new to managed futures lose money is that they have not been prepared for a drawdown. If it occurs early in the investment's cycle, they close their account and beat a retreat. Those that understand the nature of futures trading stand pat and have a better chance of prospering. We'll discuss the difference between a "buy-and-hold" strategy and market timing in Chapter 9.

At this point, let's say we have a list of five or so CTAs with minimum investment requirements of $50,000. You obtain from your broker a statistical summary of the candidates (see Exhibits 7.3 and 7.4), such as the type generated by Barclay Trading Group. Note that the second page (Exhibit 7.4) graphically illustrates the statistics on the first page (Exhibit 7.3).

As you study the information, ask yourself: "Does this CTA generate a high enough rate of return (ROR) for me to take seriously and spend a lot of time doing due diligence?" You must decide how much is enough, depending on your own situation. We also know from experience that too high a level of expectation is one of the major reason investors are unsuccessful with managed futures programs. Remember the risk-reward graph. If you expect 50 percent a year, you must be prepared to accept the volatility that goes along with extremely high returns. You'll be better off thinking about a return that is 5, 10, or 20 percent higher than what your current portfolio is making.

FIGURE 7.3

ABC TRADING CORPORATION (DIVERSIFIED)

John Doe
123 Main Street, Anytown, CA 12345
Ph. 123-456-7899   Fax 123-456-7899
1st Quarter 1994

ANNUAL RETURNS VS. BARCLAY INDEX	1989	1990	1991	1992	1993
Advisor	28.30%	43.12%	12.51%	1.84%	61.80%
Barclay Index	1.77%	21.02%	3.63%	-1.06%	10.12%
Funds Managed ($ millions)	19.5	41.8	122.6	149.8	331.2

LAST TWELVE MONTHS' PERFORMANCE VS. BARCLAY INDEX	J	F	M	A	M	J	J	A	S	O	N	D
Advisor	0.42%	15.99%	5.86%	7.38%	0.40%	0.98%	9.51%	5.84%	-2.65%	-0.07%	1.06%	5.78%
Barclay Index	-1.83%	5.46%	-0.51%	3.18%	0.62%	0.99%	3.68%	-3.02%	-0.83%	-0.61%	0.16%	2.72%

ACCOUNT INFORMATION

Management Fee:	2.00%	M/E Ratio:	20.00%
Incentive Fee:	20.00%	Options:	0.00%
Minimum Acct:	$100K	Discretion:	5.00%
RT/Yr/$ Million:	2000	Interbank:	1.00%

REWARD/RISK RATIOS

Sharpe Ratio:	0.58
Sterling Ratio:	1.32
Barclay Ratio:	0.95

TRADING METHOD

Reflects performance of the DIVERSIFIED PROGRAM, an intermediate to long term technical trend following approach.

PERFORMANCE ANALYSIS

Start Date:	01/84
Total Return Since Start Date:	2813.54%
Efficiency Index:	0.69
Compounded Average Annual ROR:	38.95%
Average Monthly ROR:	3.83%
Standard Deviation of Monthly ROR:	16.36%
Number of Winning Months: 66 Average Gain:	12.22%
Number of Losing Months: 57 Average Loss:	-5.89%
QPA:	2.93

RELATIVE VOLATILITY

Loss of 25% or more:	38.19%
Loss of 50% or more:	18.34%

DRAWDOWN REPORT				
Depth (%)	Length (Months)	Recovery (Months)	Start Date	End Date
41.8	11	3	Dec-83	Nov-84
34.5	9	6	Jul-87	Apr-88
27.4	2	3	Feb-85	Apr-85
20.6	3	2	Jul-89	Oct-89
16.6	5	2	Dec-91	May-92
15.4	9	4	Mar-86	Dec-86
9.4	3	*	Dec-93	Mar-94

TIME WINDOWS			
Length (Months)	Best	Worst	Average
1	101.26%	-27.85%	4.00%
3	165.76%	-36.13%	12.25%
6	298.02%	-38.21%	27.05%
9	551.63%	-35.33%	46.28%
12	560.95%	-33.11%	66.15%
18	768.00%	-16.13%	115.18%
24	862.69%	-2.57%	169.06%

Source: Barclay Trading Group, Ltd., Fairfield, IA.

EXHIBIT 7.4
ABC TRADING CORPORATION (DIVERSIFIED)
1st Quarter 1994

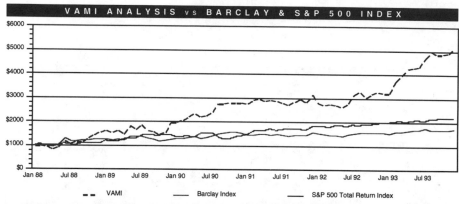

VAMI ANALYSIS vs BARCLAY & S&P 500 INDEX

- - - VAMI   —— Barclay Index   —— S&P 500 Total Return Index

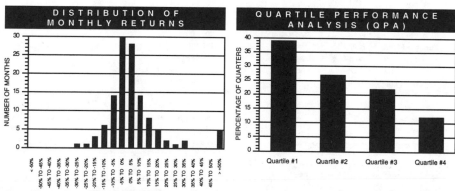

DISTRIBUTION OF MONTHLY RETURNS

QUARTILE PERFORMANCE ANALYSIS (QPA)

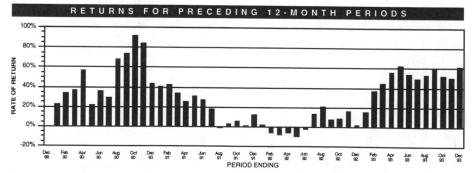

RETURNS FOR PRECEDING 12-MONTH PERIODS

Source: Barclay Trading Group, Ltd., Fairfield, IA.

86

Next, think about your long-term investment goals. As we'll document later, a buy-and-hold strategy tends to be most productive for managed futures. What level of ROR is acceptable to you over the next three to five years? You might want to zero in on a range, rather than a single figure.

Once you have a handle on the reward side of the equations, consider the risk factors. Risk is usually measured as standard deviation from the mean (average), drawdown of equity, and the various ratios (Barclay, Sharpe, Sterling, Efficiency, etc.) already discussed. Rank your CTAs using these measurements. Then think seriously about how you'll react to a drawdown in the first month you're an investor equal to the largest historical drawdown each CTA has experienced. Picture yourself sweating through that magnitude of loss. If this is more than you've bargained for, ask to see some stats on CTAs with less volatility.

We like to compare the number of winning and losing months with the average gain and loss figures. It is a method of determining the "margin of error" of each CTA's performance. For example, if one CTA has 24 winning months and 12 losing, it's a 2:1 ratio in your favor. If that same CTA's average gain is 8 percent and the loss figure is 4 percent, again you have a 2:1 ratio in your favor. Ratios like these give you some breathing room. If on the other hand, another CTA has 20 winning months and 18 losing ones with an average gain and loss of 4 percent, there is little room for error.

History tells us that whatever managed program you select, you will at some time or other experience a drawdown. What is unknown is the severity and how quickly the CTA can recover. By studying the winning/losing months ratio and the average gains/losses, you begin to get a feel for where your comfort zone is for each CTA you are considering.

You might also want to divide each CTA's compounded rate of return by his or her worst drawdown percentage. This provides another insight into how well a CTA can recover from a drawdown. Any time the result of this equation is 1 or greater, you have an excellent CTA on your hands.

Next critically study the graphs in Exhibit 7.4. Is the performance acceptable? The VAMI (Value Added Monthly Index) line should be near or above the Barclay Index and above the S&P. The "Distribution of Monthly Returns" needs to be a tight pattern to signify low volatility.

The Quartile Performance Analysis (QPA) can be very helpful in our evaluation. For example, one potential weakness of all the ratios we study is that they do not measure how a trader performed relative to the market as a whole during a particular period. But using QPA, you'd know that a 20 percent rate of return for calendar year 1989 placed a CTA in the first quartile (top 25 percent) of all active CTAs, whereas the same performance in 1987 resulted in a bottom-quartile ranking.

Using the Barclay CTA Database, Barclay Trading Group developed QPA, which indicates the percentage of calendar quarters during which a given CTA's rate of return finishes in the top quartile of all CTAs in the Barclay Index, the second quartile, and so on. The results of QPA analysis can be graphed, as in the bar charts for CTA "X" and CTA "Y" in Exhibit 7.5. These charts show the actual performance of the two CTAs over the 5-year period. Each CTA had an average compound annual return for the period of approximately 85.5 percent. Note, however, that CTA X was in the top quartile of all traders 58.3 percent of the time and in the bottom quartile only 12.5 percent of the time, whereas CTA Y, by comparison, was in the top quartile 41.7 percent of all quarters but was also in the bottom quartile 33.3 percent of the time. One can conclude that CTA Y has had a significantly greater downside volatility as indicated by the fact that one-third of the time Y's performance was in the bottom 25 percent of all traders.

An ideal profile, therefore, would show a high frequency of first- and second-quartile performance coupled with a low frequency of bottom-quartile performance. Barclay researchers have developed a single numeric indicator to show what a CTA's average quartile ranking has been over the course of his or her career. They assign four points for a first-quartile ranking, three points for a second, two points for a third-quartile ranking, and one point for a bottom-quar-

EXHIBIT 7.5

Quartile Performance Analysis

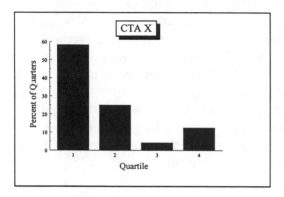

CTA X *(left)* shows an ideal profile: frequent top quartile rankings with few below-median rankings.

CTA Y *(right)* has a bi-modal distribution, including frequent high upside performance but also significant downside volatility.

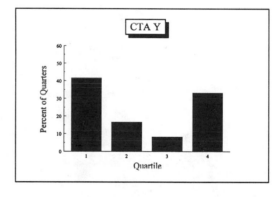

Source: Barclay Trading Group, Ltd., Fairfield, IA.

tile ranking. This indicator is termed the Barclay Quartile Performance Average (QPA). Similar to an academic grade point average system in which a 4.0 rating indicates perfect "straight A" performance, a 4.0 Barclay QPA would indicate perfect top-quartile performance in all prior quarters.

During your CTA selection process, it sometimes helps to think of hiring a CTA as you would buy an option. Your object when purchasing a call option on a stock or a futures contract is to give yourself unlimited upside potential, while limiting the downside. You do this by deciding in advance of committing to the CTA exactly what maximum loss you'll take before you bail out. Our recommendation is to limit it to the largest cumulative drawdown the CTA has ever experienced. If he or she exceeds this amount, you're out! Or, if that amount is too high, don't invest in the first place.

It is critical to develop or adopt analytical tools that will make you comfortable with your decisions, so that you will be prepared to stay with your advisors to reap the rewards that are available from professionally managed futures trading accounts.

8

How Much Can You (or Should You) Rely on the Statistical Analysis?

The more time you spend with your nose in disclosure documents, the more you'll encounter the following statement: "Past performance is not indicative of future results." The CFTC requires this warning to be prominently displayed near every CTA's performance table.

It only means that, if a CTA made money yesterday, there is no guarantee he or she will do it today. Very little in life is guaranteed. Why should we expect more from someone trading our money in a very volatile environment, such as the futures market—or even the stock market for that matter?

The reason for the insistence of the CFTC on a conspicuous display of this declaration is that those who promote CTAs, which can often be the CTA him- or herself, have little else to use to convince you to invest in their program. Conversely, a CTA's past performance is usually the first thing an investor asks to see when he or she becomes interested in a CTA. For these reasons, it is important to gauge just how far you can rely on statistical analysis in general and a track record in particular.

The CFTC requires a CTA to disclose the last three years of performance in a disclosure document. If you know the CTA has traded longer than three years, you'll want to inquire about why only three years are included. The missing data, if available, might change many of the statistics, such as longest and deepest drawdown or percentage of profitable months. In general, the more data you have, the more reliable the numbers you generate.

Some CTAs would like to lose or forget about their early trading. This is understandable and even forgivable. Hopefully, the longer a person trades, the better they get. Also, new or emerging CTAs often feel compelled to be extremely aggressive traders. They must make their mark quickly in order to attract investors and press coverage.

At the same time, they may just be developing their own trading system. Even the best have bugs. Working them out can be expensive in time and trading equity. Additionally, the trader may not have a lot of money under management. This means that any drawdown of equity is serious. For example, if a trader with $100,000 under management loses $5,000 in silver, it's a 5 percent drawdown. But if this trader is managing $1 million, the same loss represents only one half of 1 percent.

Apply this same line of reasoning when studying early winnings as well. What would be small, insignificant gains by a CTA with millions in tow could be barn-burner percentage increases for a little guy. Look at percentages, but keep them in perspective. One way to do this is by charting 3-month time windows of the ROR, for example, over the early and later years of trading. If the return figures improve, it is a good sign.

Another thing to look for in a track record is notional fund tables. Notional funds are not the same as real or regular equity. It is pledged or promised money. An investor deposits $50,000 with a CTA and tells him or her to trade it as if it were $100,000. If the CTA would normally risk no more than 50 percent at any one time, he or she can trade with 100 percent—one-half real and one-half notional.

Notional trading performance tables must be labeled as such. It would show cash deposited as $50,000 and notional equity as $100,000. If the trader made a $5,000 profit for the first month, the ROR would be 10 percent for cash and 5 percent for notional equity.

Notional equity increases the amount of dollars being traded. The amount kept in reserve is reduced. This does two things. First, it increases the amount of leverage of the account. As mentioned earlier, CTAs routinely hold half of each investor's equity in reserve. Twenty-five thousand dollars could be traded in a futures portfolio like the one below.

Diversified Futures Portfolio

Commodity	$ Value	Margin
Live Cattle	$24,000.00 (40,000 lb. × 60¢)	$800.00
Corn	$13,500.00 (5,000 bu. × $2.70)	$500.00
CRB Index	$112,500.00 (500 × $225.00)	$2,000.00
Gold	$38,000.00 (100 oz. × $380/oz.)	$2,000.00
Crude Oil	$18,000.00 (1,000 bbl. × $18.00)	$1,500.00
Swiss Franc	$25,000.00 (125,000 × 20¢)	$2,200.00
Wheat	$20,000.00 (5,000 bu. × $4.00)	$500.00
T-Bonds	$50,000.00 (Face Value)	$1,100.00
Soybean Meal	$25,000.00 (100 tons × $250.00)	$1,000.00
Sugar	$11,200.00 (112,000 lbs. × 10¢)	$700.00
U.S. Dollar Index	$100,000.00 (1,000 × $100.00)	$2,000.00
Totals	$437,200.00	$14,300.00

To reach the approximate $25,000 equity position, two contracts of each commodity would be traded.

Leverage Factor

$ Value of Portfolio = $ Value × Number of Contracts

= $437,200.00 × 2

= $874,400.00

$$\text{Leverage} = \text{Margin Money} \div \$ \text{ Value}$$
$$= \$28,600.00(\$14,300.00 \times 2) \div \$874,400.00$$
$$= 3.3\%$$

In this example, less than $30,000 is controlling almost $900,000 of commodities. If the CTA used an additional $50,000 in notional funds, the investor would be controlling over a million and a half dollars of commodities with a $50,000 investment.

The profit potential of this much leveraging is astounding. It is what attracts aggressive investors. The risk can be equally catastrophic. It is for this reason so much emphasis is placed on survival and drawdown management. If a CTA can manage the risk, he or she can be in position at some time or other to capitalize on the potential.

The dollar amounts of the margin money required to hold each position are only representative. They are changed periodically, depending on market conditions, by the Margin Committee of each exchange, which meets daily. The primary factor is the current volatility of the contract. The higher the volatility, the higher the margin.

When studying a performance table that includes a notional column, pay particular attention to the ROR of the notional equity. This provides a more meaningful insight into the performance of a typical account.

You should also carefully consider if you want to invest with a CTA that trades notional funds. Some investors consider this practice as a Macro-Disqualifier. They believe there is risk enough without increasing the leverage to the brink. There is no definitive answer that suits everyone. We caution you to always pay close attention to those statistics, already discussed, that attempt to quantify risk control.

Quartile Performance Analysis

The question of how much to rely on past performance can be addressed by Barclay's Quartile Performance Analysis, used in the previous chapter in the CTA selection process. For example, a track record is created based on certain market conditions, which may or may not ever be repeated. Even if similar conditions occur, the trader may or may not recognize them or trade them the same way. Additionally, few professionals can wait for just the right price patterns to trade. If they did, they'd do so few trades their performance would be meaningless.

Barclay Trading Group decided to test whether there is any serial correlation over extended periods of time between a CTA's earlier and later performance. They focused on the change in a CTA's relative performance over an extended period of time, relative to the performance of a large population of CTAs.

Their methodology included the use of two performance indicators as measures of comparison: (1) each CTA's average annual return, and (2) the ratio of average monthly return to the standard deviation of monthly returns. The first measures reward, while the second compares the reward-to-risk relationship. Both of these evaluation measures are widely used and are nonarbitrary in design.

Next, they selected a group of 145 trading advisors. This population included all the CTAs from the Barclay CTA Database who traded continuously throughout a three-year period at the time of the study. Thirty-two of the original 145 went out of business during the second three-year period, leaving 113.

They ranked by quartile all 145 CTAs by each of the two performance criteria during each of the two three-year periods. Actually, for the second period they ranked the 113 surviving CTAs by quartile and had a fifth "out of business" category. Finally, they compared the change in each CTA's relative ranking from the first three-year period to the second. As the accompanying exhibits indicate, the results are quite interesting.

When comparing change in relative rank by average annual return (see Exhibits 8.1 and 8.2), the following results emerge. Forty-three of the 145 CTAs measured (29.7 percent) achieved the same quartile ranking during the second three-year period as they had in the first. If the "out of business" category is added to the bottom quartile for the second period, this figure increases to 56 CTAs (38.6 percent).

EXHIBIT 8.1

Average Annual Return

January 1986 to December 1988

		Quartile 1	Quartile 2	Quartile 3	Quartile 4
	Quartile 1	12	5	3	8
Jan '89	Quartile 2	8	10	7	4
to					
Dec '91	Quartile 3	3	6	12	6
	Quartile 4	7	6	7	9
	Out of Business	7	6	6	13

Source: Barclay Trading Group, Ltd., Fairfield, IA.

An additional 39 CTAs had their relative ranking move up or down one quartile (e.g., top quartile in first period and second quartile in second period). As a result, a total of 95 of the 145 CTAs (65.1 percent) had performance shifts in one quartile or less.

The remaining 50 CTAs, including those who ceased operations, had shifts of two or three quartiles. Only 22 firms (15.2 percent) experienced the maximum three-quartile shift.

The results for the reward-to-risk rankings (see Exhibits 8.3 and 8.4) are very similar: 64.1 percent of the CTAs experienced a shift of one quartile or less, and only 17 firms (11.7 percent) experienced a three-quartile shift.

EXHIBIT 8.2

Average Annual Return Results

	Number of CTAs	Percent of CTAs
Same Quartile Ranking	43	29.7%
Moved Up/Down 1 Quartile	39	26.9%
Moved Up/Down 2 or More Quartiles	31	21.4%
Out of Business	32	22.1%

Source: Barclay Trading Group, Ltd., Fairfield, IA.

The results seem to indicate a slight positive serial correlation over the two time periods of relative performance rankings. Had there been no correlation between earlier and later performance, the outcome would have been a random distribution with an equal number of CTAs in each of the boxes.

It is important to note that eight of the 36 CTAs who were in the top quartile during the first three-year period subsequently went out of business during the second period, while another five finished in the bottom quartile the second time around. The distribution is random enough to prove that "Past performance is not necessarily indicative of future results."

EXHIBIT 8.3

Average Monthly Return/
Standard Deviation of Return

January 1986 to December 1988

		Quartile 1	Quartile 2	Quartile 3	Quartile 4
	Quartile 1	13	6	3	6
Jan '89 to Dec '91	Quartile 2	6	10	6	7
	Quartile 3	3	6	13	5
	Quartile 4	6	7	7	9
	Out of Business	5	7	8	12

Source: Barclay Trading Group, Ltd., Fairfield, IA.

Seeing the Forest from the Trees

Try not to get so wrapped up in sophisticated statistical analysis that you overlook the more mundane red flags. If your advisory service is small, basically a one-person operation, he or she could get sick, injured, or distracted from the market by personal problems. Be sure there is some backup, like a good broker, who can step in and close out open positions.

You should even pay attention to the back office portion of the business. This refers to record keeping, order execution, and accounting. If any of these break down, so does the entire operation. Sloppy

EXHIBIT 8.4

Reward-to-Risk Results

	Number of CTAs	Percent of CTAs
Same Quartile Ranking	45	31.0%
Moved Up/Down 1 Quartile	36	24.8%
Moved Up/Down 2 or More Quartiles	32	22.1%
Out of Business	32	21.1%

Source: Barclay Trading Group, Ltd., Fairfield, IA.

back office procedures can also bring down the wrath of the NFA, CFTC, and exchanges.

More importantly, a solid administrative function assures that accounts are closely monitored. Are all positions accounted for? Is the leverage percentage correct by account and for the entire portfolio? This is one of the key control factors in risk management.

Due to the volume of trades, which can easily be in the hundreds or thousands each day, there is always the chance something will go wrong. An order to go long 100 contracts of heating oil could be called in as a short. Sloppy handwriting by the order desk clerk at the exchange might result in an order for June T-bills to be read as December. When the fill is called back to the CTA's order desk, it must be caught and corrected. Each day every order must be reconciled.

When you visit your trader, observe the back office carefully. We like to see that all calls made to the exchanges are tape-recorded, so they can be checked if there is any reason to suspect an error. The exchange tapes all calls, but often cannot replay them until after the trading session is over. That's too late if an erroneous trade is in the market.

At the end of each day, the clearing firm wires to the CTA a computer run of all the trades he or she did on that day. It must be carefully checked and filed. You may want to look at past copies to make sure these preliminary runs are checked and approved. Any changes or corrections are immediately called to the clearing firm's attention and a final run is transmitted before the beginning of the next day's trading.

Besides these two runs, it is even better if trade confirmations are wired to the CTA throughout the day, as they are inputted into the clearing firm's computer. More advanced systems give traders direct access to the computer files. They can check, via a remote computer terminal, when a trade is put on the system and if it is correct. This real-time capability enhances any back office operation. The enormous amount of leverage and the volatility of the futures market magnifies the fear of errors.

Be sure to evaluate the idle cash management system used by your CTA. The better systems sweep any dollars not being used for margin into an interest-bearing account. Some do not pay interest to customers. Historically, discount brokerage firms made a goodly portion of their profits from the interest income generated by customers' idle cash.

Ask some questions and carefully observe to determine if the CTA or one or more of his or her assistants is a detail person. Without a detail fanatic, there is no way to keep all the paperwork required for the business straight.

9

The Value and Risk of
Market Timing Strategies

In an attempt to deal with the randomness of forecasting the future, many investors have attempted to develop market timing strategies. We alluded to this in Chapter 4 with regard to stocks. Now we'd specifically like to address the question of switching between CTAs.

You might analyze the futures market, for example, and come to the conclusion that there is a major bull market developing in the grains, metals, currencies, or whatever. You'd then sort through your database of CTAs to select the best possible choices specializing in the appropriate commodity group. Another common dilemma for investors is whether to invest, or increase an investment, in a CTA when he or she is in a drawdown or an upswing.

The practice of buying after a decline in value is generally recognized as a contrarian strategy and has had a number of eloquent proponents. One of the most notable is Dr. Douglas G. Mitchell, Ph.D., founder and president of CCA Capital Management, Inc. CCA is a trend-following CTA firm based in Delmar, New York. Dr. Mitchell argues that when investing with trend-following CTAs, risk-adjusted performance may be enhanced by hiring or investing more during drawdowns and systematically withdrawing profits during runups.

If an investor believes that a CTA's prior performance is predictive of what his or her future performance will be, then pinpointing that CTA's "low" and "high" is relatively easy. If, as an extreme example, an investor believes that a CTA will never exceed his or her prior worst drawdown, then a market timing strategy makes impeccable sense. Such a strategy would clearly indicate that the investor should "buy" whenever the CTA approaches that theoretical drawdown "floor." Why? Because the only way to go from there is up—theoretically, of course.

The opposite strategy also has its adherents. At a MAR/MFA Mid-Year Conference on Futures Money Management in Chicago, Mr. Monroe Trout of Trout Trading Company suggested that superior results may in fact be achieved by investing with CTAs who are showing positive performance trends, as opposed to those who have just sustained losses. This approach is more akin to the classic strategy of cutting your losses and letting your winners run. E. H. Harriman summarized this strategy when he said, "If you want to make money in stocks, kill your losses." When applied to managed futures, this does not imply that physical violence is the appropriate way to deal with a CTA who has incurred a loss, although some have considered it. It does, however, suggest that investing more during a drawdown may not be as effective as adding during a positive move.

If this is not confusing enough, there is yet a third alternative—"buy and hold" for the long run without respect to whether a CTA is currently in a drawdown or a runup. The buy-and-hold approach does not imply that CTA selection is random or indiscriminate; rather, it suggests that after carefully selecting a CTA based upon thorough due diligence, an investor may invest without regard to market timing issues or waiting for an appropriate time "window" to invest. Or, if an investor believes that CTA performance is strictly random and that past performance has no serial correlation with future performance, then a market timing strategy makes little sense. Just because a CTA had just experienced the worst drawdown of his or her career is no guarantee that it would not be followed by a continuing loss.

In fact, many CTAs have terminated their trading activities following drawdowns worse than any they had previously experienced. The market timing strategy applied in these cases would only have resulted in losses.

The Buy-and-Hold Strategy

What reasons would suggest that a buy-and-hold strategy might yield superior results when compared to timing strategies? Buy-and-hold proponents argue that the most important factor to consider is that market timing approaches inevitably will cause the investor to be "out of the market" for periods of time. If the investor participates in limited partnerships, even a switch from one fund to another may cause the investor's capital to be on the sidelines for a month or more. The very periods in which the market timing system has caused the investor to disinvest may result in the "loss" of substantial gains that would have occurred. In fact, as these proponents argue, gains in managed futures often occur in a very concentrated fashion during a relatively few and unpredictable periods of time.

A look at industry history tends to confirm this position. During the period from January 1980 to June 1992, the Barclay CTA Index experienced only 13 months with gains of 10 percent or more. However, those 13 double-digit months accounted for *two-thirds of the total index profitability* during the period (a 629.3 percent gain during the 13 months compared to the total period return of 931.2 percent). Take those 13 months away and the compound annual return for the managed futures industry for the period drops from 21.46 percent to 12.29 percent.

How likely is it that a market timing approach would have anticipated those periods of high profitability so as to be "in the market" at the right time? Exhibit 9.1 lists each of the double-digit gaining months and shows the performance of the Barclay CTA Index for the three-month and six-month periods prior to and following each

EXHIBIT 9.1
Analysis of Largest Gaining Months

January 1980 – June 1992

Month	Barclay CTA Index Monthly Performance	Barclay CTA Index Performance Prior to and Following Gaining Month			
		6 Mos. Prior	3 Mos. Prior	3 Mos. Post	6 Mos. Post
Jan 80	+29.35%	N.A.	N.A.	+2.94%	+22.33%
Jul 80	+11.29%	+42.30%	+4.71%	+3.54%	+8.65%
Jun 81	+16.62%	+7.33%	+1.09%	−2.54%	−0.93%
Jan 83	+18.94%	−5.24%	−8.60%	−8.09%	−4.76%
May 83	+10.05%	+8.69%	−8.09%	+2.67%	+0.14%
Jul 84	+21.45%	−5.66%	−8.22%	−8.30%	−1.93%
Jul 85	+13.89%	+0.72%	−5.24%	−3.36%	+11.37%
Feb 86	+14.25%	+11.37%	+15.24%	−4.65%	+2.05%
Jan 87	+10.45%	−4.27%	−6.70%	+27.10%	+26.12%
Apr 87	+22.11%	+7.25%	+14.96%	−0.78%	−1.44%
Jun 88	+26.69%	+3.62%	+0.46%	−6.77%	−4.45%
May 89	+11.70%	+0.56%	−2.52%	−6.16%	−12.28%
Dec 91	+10.04%	−0.60%	+2.18%	−8.31%	−4.80%
Average	+5.50%	−0.06%	−0.98%	+3.08%	
Total Number Positive	8	6	4	6	
Total Number Negative	4	6	9	7	

Source: Barclay Trading Group, Ltd., Fairfield, IA.

of the major gaining months. A contrarian would expect that the large gaining months might follow drawdown periods. The contrarian might also expect a drawdown to follow such large positive moves. On the other hand, the noncontrarian might expect a major upmove to follow a period of positive results.

What Barclay Trading Group Found

Barclay's research indicates that the timing of major gaining months is quite random. As Exhibit 9.1 demonstrates, of the six-month periods prior to the upmoves, eight were positive and four were negative. The six-month windows following a major gain were also evenly split—six positive and seven negative. Only the three-month windows immediately following a major gain would lend support to the contrarian viewpoint—nine were negative and only four positive, suggesting that selling following a runup might make sense.

The risk inherent in a market timing approach, therefore, may be that in the attempt to minimize volatility one misses a major profitable move. Their findings suggest that the performance of the managed futures industry is not so much *cyclical* as it is *random*. This randomness makes it very difficult to predict exactly when a major move to the upside will occur.

The random occurrence of major positive moves is logical when one considers the variety of factors that can lead to trends in the commodity and financial futures markets. The double-digit move in December 1991, for example, was primarily attributable to the Federal Reserve Bank's reduction in the discount rate. The June 1988 gain, on the other hand, was in large part due to the U.S. drought's impact on agricultural prices. In fact, major trends could be caused by factors as diverse as the weather, central bank intervention in the currency markets, changes in inflation or in primary economic indicators, or the stock market, to name but a few. It could be argued that each of these factors is cyclical within itself, but most observers would agree that the combined multivariable influence of all the factors taken together is random in nature. In light of these findings, the buy-and-hold strategy deserves serious consideration as an approach to managed futures investing over long periods of time.

Next, Barclay Trading Group attempted to zero in on more specific periods of time immediately following major upturns or drawdowns of CTAs on their database. Would this give any additional insight to timing?

To answer this question, they studied the individual perform-ance results of a large population of CTAs during two five-year time periods—one ending December 31, 1991, and the other ending De-cember 31, 1992. They examined two different periods because the first five-year period began with a generally profitable quarter for most CTAs, whereas the second five-year period did not. One hun-dred ninety CTA programs were examined during the first period and 244 were included in the second. All had at least one year of performance history prior to the beginning of the period.

Their findings include the results of CTAs who went out of business during the five-year research periods. This is important to note, because if you examine the performance of only those CTAs who survived the five-year periods, the results obtained are very different—and very misleading.

Measuring Buy-and-Hold

In order to measure the results of a buy-and-hold strategy during each period, they measured the cumulative five-year return achieved by investing an equal amount of money with each CTA at the begin-ning of the period and holding that investment for five years—or until a CTA went out of business. After a CTA went out of business, the remaining investment capital was assumed to earn the current T-bill rate for the duration of the five-year period.

Measuring Market Timing

Measuring the results of market timing strategies was not quite so easy. First, they needed to determine which market timing approach yielded the best results. So, for each period they tested the results of "buying" each individual CTA following drawdowns of 10 percent through 50 percent at 10 percent increments and "selling" each CTA following runups of 10 percent through 100 percent, again at 10 per-cent increments. They also examined each of these approaches under two scenarios—assuming that the investor's initial position was "in the market," i.e., fully invested with each CTA, and "out of the market," i.e., no investment was made until the appropriate drawdown occurred.

During all periods in which the investor was "out of the market," i.e., not invested with a particular CTA, that amount of investment capital was assumed to earn the current T-bill rate.

Comparing the Results

As can be seen from the table in Exhibit 9.2, the buy-and-hold strategy yielded a total return of 176.86 percent for the five years ending December 31, 1991, and 70.66 percent for the five years ending December 31, 1992. The results of the various market timing approaches are graphically displayed in the charts in Exhibits 9.3 and 9.4.

The two charts require some explaining. In each, the horizontal axis indicates the size of the runup causing the investor to sell or disinvest from a CTA. The vertical axis shows the cumulative return achieved from the strategy. The graphed lines show the results obtained by investing after different-sized drawdowns.

EXHIBIT 9.2

Strategy Analysis
Buy-and-Hold vs. Market Timing

	1/1/87 to 12/31/91		1/1/88 to 12/31/92	
	Total Return	S.D. of Returns	Total Return	S.D. of Returns
Buy-and-Hold	176.86%	±271.48%	70.66%	±117.66%
"Best" Timing Strategy	192.58%	±328.51%	79.73%	±114.45%

Source: Barclay Trading Group, Ltd., Fairfield, IA.

EXHIBIT 9.3

Buy-and-Hold vs. Market Timing Strategies

Results of 190 CTAs for the period 1/1/87 to 12/31/91

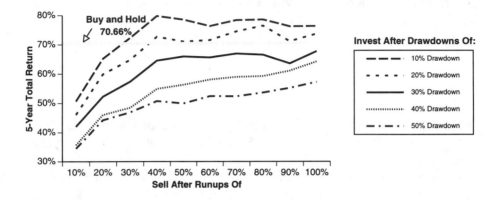

Source: Barclay Trading Group, Ltd., Fairfield, IA.

During each time period, the optimal market timing approaches involved investing with a CTA following a small rather than a large drawdown and disinvesting following a large rather than a small runup. Also, it was more effective to begin "in the market" rather than to wait for a drawdown to occur.

Of the 100 market timing approaches tested during each time period, a few yielded returns higher than the buy-and-hold approach, but many of these also had higher standard deviations of returns. What is most striking is the fact that the market timing strategies that proved to be the most effective were those that were most similar to a buy-and-hold approach, i.e., buy after a small drawdown and sell after a large runup. This type of strategy results in the investor being "in the market" nearly as much as a buy-and-hold approach. The opposite approach—i.e., buying after a large drawdown and selling after a large runup—results in the investor's money being invested in T-bills a large portion of the time and yields much lower rates of return.

EXHIBIT 9.4

Buy-and-Hold vs. Market Timing Strategies

Results of 244 CTAs for the period 1/1/88 to 12/31/92

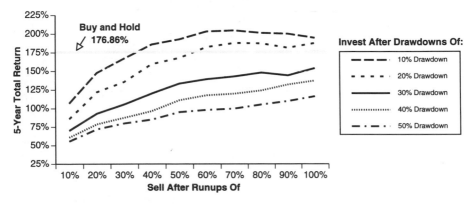

Source: Barclay Trading Group, Ltd., Fairfield, IA.

In summary, a small percentage of market timing strategies may yield returns that exceed buy-and-hold approaches. The incremental gains, however, are small and, when considered on a risk-adjusted basis, may be insignificant. As mentioned earlier, Barclay theorized that a potential drawback to market timing approaches may be that they cause an investor to "miss" major gaining periods while the investor was "out" of the market. This seems to be confirmed by this study. Another argument to consider in favor of buy-and-hold is the sentiment that if CTA cycles were indeed predictable and amenable to market timing approaches, the CTAs themselves would have already incorporated cycles into their money management practices and altered their trading accordingly.

In short, the test results seem to indicate that a long-term perspective toward managed futures investments can yield the best results over time. A buy-and-hold approach is also easier to implement and involves lower switching costs.

10

Some Miscellaneous Concerns Regarding CTA Performance

By now, you should have a pretty good feel for sizing up CTAs based on their stats. In this chapter, we'd like to discuss some other issues you should be aware of, in case you ever have to deal with them.

The question of whether trading advisor performance deteriorates as money under management increases is an important issue facing the managed futures industry today. The answer, however, is neither obvious nor easy to define.

Meaningful answers have proven to be elusive because "performance" can be measured in a variety of ways. Absolute performance, as defined in terms of annual rates of return, may not be an accurate or useful indicator of trading success for two reasons.

First, even though a trading advisor's rates of return may decline over a period of years as assets under management increase, the CTA's volatility or risk exposure may also decrease. As a result, "performance," when defined in terms of the reward/risk relationship, may actually improve even though absolute return declines.

The second difficulty in comparing performance versus money under management is how to take into account the effect of variations in market conditions from one year to the next.

For example, as Exhibit 10.1 indicates, the performance of the Barclay CTA Index has varied widely over the years. As a result, in order to adequately assess the performance of an individual CTA in a given year, one must consider not only absolute performance, but also performance relative to all other trading advisors during that year. For example, a rate of return of 10 percent in 1987 would have indicated relatively modest performance, whereas a 20 percent return during 1989 would have ranked a CTA among the industry's leaders.

In order to determine whether CTA performance changes with increasing assets while taking into account this "market effect," we asked Barclay Trading Group to research the question. They decided to select a diversified group of CTAs who had significantly increased assets under management over four years and to measure their annual performance relative to the performance of all other CTAs in the Barclay CTA Index.

The universe of CTAs for this study included all CTA programs that met the following criteria:

- The CTA program had traded continuously since January 1, 1987.

- Assets under management at least doubled in the three-year period between December 31, 1987, and December 31, 1990.

EXHIBIT 10.1

Barclay CTA Index Annual Returns

1987	57.31%
1988	20.11%
1989	2.19%
1990	21.82%

Source: Barclay Trading Group, Ltd., Fairfield, IA.

- Total assets under management as of December 31, 1990, were at least $50 million. Some of the CTA firms offered more than one trading program.

A total of 26 CTA programs met the criteria. The names of these programs and their amounts of money managed at the end of each calendar year from 1987 through 1990 are listed in Exhibit 10.2. The combined assets managed by this group increased from $893 million at the end of 1987 to more than $4.5 billion at the end of 1990, an increase of approximately 410 percent.

During that same three-year period the managed futures industry as a whole increased from approximately $8 billion at December 31, 1987, to an estimated $20 billion at December 31, 1990, a gain of 150 percent. If the select group's growth is eliminated from this calculation, the rest of the industry grew by less than 120 percent during the three-year period. As a result, the select group of 26 CTAs grew at almost three and one-half times the industry as a whole.

The next task was to determine the performance of this select group relative to the rest of the CTA industry in each year. To do this, they used their Quartile Performance Average (QPA) technique, described earlier. This procedure measures how often a CTA's quarterly rate of return ranks in each quartile when compared to quarterly returns for all CTAs. The top quartile includes the top 25 percent of all CTAs; the second quartile includes the next 25 percent, etc.

As you may remember, they assign 4 points for a top-quartile finish, 3 points for the second, 2 points for third, and 1 point for a bottom-quartile ranking. They then take an average of the point total and term it the Quartile Performance Average (QPA). Similar to an academic grade point average, the QPA is a single number that indicates how well a CTA has performed relative to all other CTAs over the term of his or her trading career. For example, a 4.0 QPA is a "perfect" score, indicating a top-quartile ranking in each quarter of the CTA's career. A 1.0 QPA would indicate consistent bottom-quartile rankings, while a 2.5 QPA would indicate median performance.

EXHIBIT 10.2

Growth of Assets under Management

Amounts in Millions of Dollars as of Each Year-End

	Trading Advisor	1987	1988	1989	1990
1.	Adam, Harding, & Lueck	11.7	48.7	24.6	85.0
2.	AZF Commodity Management	10.8	17.1	53.9	98.0
3.	Beacon Management Corp.	22.6	47.8	43.4	57.2
4.	Blenheim Investments, Inc.	14.5	51.3	171.5	324.8
5.	Campbell & Co. (Currency)	0.1	21.4	29.0	110.0
6.	Chang-Crowell (Diversified)	55.7	104.0	81.2	115.0
7.	Desai & Co.	72.6	127.0	151.8	175.0
8.	Dunn Capital (World Monetary)	8.9	15.5	34.9	150.0
9.	ELM Financial, Inc.	12.6	44.0	99.8	119.1
10.	John W. Henry (Fin. & Metals)	15.2	36.9	68.8	279.8
11.	LaSalle Portfolio Management	10.3	34.8	82.0	85.0
12.	Little Brook Corp. of N.J.	60.9	204.0	136.8	98.2
13.	Mint Investment Mgmt. Corp.	304.2	715.0	922.0	955.0
14.	Tom Mitchell, CTA	12.9	54.2	114.0	152.0
15.	Moore Capital Management	23.3	42.9	95.0	300.0
16.	Rabar Market Research	1.2	2.6	18.5	65.0
17.	Reynwood Trading Corp.	6.6	53.2	69.5	119.2
18.	RXR, Inc. (Balanced Program)	3.7	3.8	52.4	219.0
19.	RXR, Inc. (Mark III)	7.1	7.4	16.6	51.1
20.	Sabre Fund Management Ltd.	30.4	73.4	74.5	97.0
21.	Saxon Investment Corp.	5.0	1.6	25.3	70.0
22.	Spackenkill Trading Co.	9.2	16.6	26.5	52.0
23.	Sunrise Commodities (Diver.)	20.0	26.1	35.3	62.7
24.	Trout Trading Co.	1.9	2.6	52.0	192.4
25.	Tudor Investment Corp.	158.0	171.7	385.0	466.0
26.	Willowbridge Assoc. (Vulcan)	13.7	64.2	41.6	55.2
	Select Group Totals:	893.1			4,553.7

Source: Barclay Trading Group, Ltd., Fairfield, IA.

Findings and Conclusions

They measured the combined QPA of the select group of 26 CTAs for each of the years 1987 through 1990. They also compared the select group's combined average performance during each year to the Barclay CTA Index. The results are contained in Exhibit 10.3.

Because they were attempting to measure change in performance relative to assets managed as compared to the industry as a whole, they were less interested in the absolute numbers in a single year than in the trend from one year to the next.

As indicated in Exhibit 10.3, the select group's QPA was higher in 1989 and 1990 than it had been in 1987 or 1988, indicating a general improvement in performance relative to the industry as a whole. As can also be seen, the select group's combined average annual rates of return also significantly outperformed the Barclay CTA Index in each year except 1988.

Clearly this type of research needs to be conducted over longer periods of time and with larger sample sizes as more CTAs achieve substantial amounts of assets under management. Nonetheless, this QPA research indicates that the common knowledge on the street that performance declines as assets increase is perhaps not so accurate. In fact, it appears that the industry's largest and most rapidly growing CTAs have outperformed the rest of the industry, when accounting for relative market conditions, by widening margins.

EXHIBIT 10.3

Select CTA Group Annual Performance

	1987	1988	1989	1990
Combined QPA	2.52	2.66	2.85	2.73
Average 1-Year Return	68.88%	15.92%	17.78%	31.0%
Average 1-Year Return vs. Barclay CTA Index	+11.57%	−4.19%	+15.59%	+9.19%

Source: Barclay Trading Group, Ltd., Fairfield, IA.

There are also some psychological factors to consider. Some successful CTAs become conservative. This can happen on almost any level. After trading and sales have gone well for a while, they are in control of several millions of dollars. This money produces a very decent living just from the management fee, not to mention any incentive bonuses. The CTA begins to think of himself as a manager, rather than a futures trader.

Equally deadly to a futures trader is the inordinate fear of loss that can build up after one has been trading for a while. It's not unlike a soldier's response to a combat situation. It's easy to be brave and fearless until you see a comrade in arms fall to enemy fire. All of a sudden, it's for real. Some traders have difficulty overcoming their first major drawdown. We prefer to invest with someone who has passed this milestone.

You'll also encounter traders who have problems "pulling the trigger." This can mean entering or exiting trades. Strange as it may seem, some CTAs can do one or the other very well, but not both. You weed out these guys by doing your statistical analysis first and walking away from hypothetical track record presentations. If it's not real life, it's not worth investigating.

Fees

Fees can be a stumbling block, a Macro-Disqualifier. As mentioned earlier, most CTAs require a management fee based on the amount of money under management. It can range from 2 percent to 6 percent per year, paid monthly or quarterly.

Next, they'll ask for an incentive fee of 10 percent to 25 percent. The incentive fee is usually a percentage of what are called new trading profits earned each period (month, quarter). New profits means new net gains. For example, if an account begins a quarter with $100,000 and ends that quarter with $120,000, with the $20,000 being trading profits, the CTA receives an incentive on the $20,000. Now, if the account loses $5,000 the second quarter, dropping to

$115,000, no incentive is paid. Nor is any incentive paid until the account once again exceeds $120,000. If there is a third-quarter net gain of $15,000, the CTA earns an incentive on $10,000, which is the new profit ($115,000 + $15,000 − $120,000).

Last of all are the brokerage fees. They cover the cost of actually executing the trades, clearing them (back office on several levels), paying brokers (if one is involved), plus fees to the NFA and the appropriate exchanges. Brokerage fees are charged on a per trade basis and are known as trailing commissions because they trail behind the account as long as it trades. The normal range can be anywhere from $10 to $100 per round turn, which includes initiating a trade and later offsetting it.

A typical $50 round-turn commission would break out something like this. First of all, the NFA and exchange fees would be additional to the basic $50 rate charge. They would run anywhere from $1.50 to $2.50, depending on which exchange is used. New York exchanges tend to be a little more expensive than other places, such as Chicago, Kansas City, or Minneapolis.

Of the $50, approximately $10 to $15 would be used to pay the clearing corporations, the floor broker and his or her company, and the cost of handling all the paperwork. The remaining $15 to $40 goes to the brokerage firm that opened the account. This is another way of saying they sold the investment program to an investor. The individual broker who actually did the selling receives 20 percent to 30 percent of this amount. The other 70 percent to 80 percent is used by the broker of record's company for sales, marketing, administration, and contribution to overhead.

Naturally, it is to your advantage to find or negotiate the lowest fees. But don't throw the baby out with the bath water! Your objective is to find the best trader you possibly can. Fees are extremely important, but the best traders and brokers, as with the best of any profession, are expensive. It's far better to pay higher fees and make money, than to lose money at a lower brokerage rate. Negotiate, but don't be stupid.

Key Questions to Ask about Fees

1. Are there National Futures Association and exchange fees in addition to the brokerage fees?

2. How much is the brokerage commission?

3. Is the fee charged when a trade is put on, half when put on and half when offset, or all when offset?

4. Are brokerage commissions on options or futures charged any differently?

5. Approximately how many round-turn trades are done per $1 million under management per year? (This is a commonly calculated figure, which you can use to figure out your monthly brokerage cost. Or, you can simply ask how many trades per month would normally be done in an account of the size you plan on opening.)

6. How is the management fee computed?

7. How is it paid? Is it deducted directly from the account or billed to the brokerage firm by the CTA?

8. How much is the incentive fee? Is it on new profits? If idle funds are held in interest-bearing accounts, is the earned interest included in the incentive?

9. Which fees does the CTA share in? Management? Incentive? Brokerage? (It is usually considered bad form for the CTA to share in the brokerage commission, since it encourages as much trading as possible.)

10. Are there any additional fees (accounting, purchase of T-bills, administration, upfront sales commissions) you should be aware of?

11. If more than one CTA trades the account on the fund, can one or more of the CTAs earn an incentive even if the fund does not generate new profits in a given period?

12. Which fees are negotiable? Management? Incentive? Brokerage? Will the CTA agree to a higher incentive fee only if the performance exceeds an agreed-upon rate of return?

11

Psychological Aspects of CTA Selection

You need to be concerned with the psychological aspects of investing in a managed futures program from two distinct points of view. First, what type of investment best meets your needs? And second, if you're going to personally interview and select a CTA, what psychological characteristics should you be looking for?

The type of futures investment you are suited for depends on your attitude toward risk. If you are an aggressive risk-taker, you might be looking for an emerging CTA with a short, but incredible, track record. A moderate risk-taker might select a seasoned trader with a five- to ten-year track record in the moderate volatility range. Safety-conscious investors prefer to define their maximum risk in advance. They look for limited partnerships and "guaranteed" funds. We'll have a discussion of the various types of offerings later in this text.

If you're not sure of where you fit in the risk-reward spectrum, consider getting a copy of *Your Inner Path to Investment Success: In-*

sights into the Psychology of Investing, by Dr. Albert Mehrabian (Probus Publishing Company, 1991).

Dr. Mehrabian matches personality types to investments. First you pinpoint your personality and then you look for investments that are suited to that personality type. His theory is that investments can be classified based on the amount of uncertainty involved in their forecasted results. A certificate of deposit in a federally insured bank is secure. Bankrolling an unproven commodity trader is capricious at best.

To sort out personality types of investors, Dr. Mehrabian first divides temperaments into pleasant and unpleasant. The focal point is your social expectation. Are you an optimist or pessimist? Do you expect every investment to generate returns beyond your expectations or do you always fear loss of capital? When you pour whisky into a tumbler of water, are you improving the water or ruining the scotch? The more optimistic an investor is, the more likely one is to take risks.

Next, you quantify your response to emotional stimuli. Are you aroused easily or do you consider yourself unemotional? Highly excited people talk with their hands, are very animated, and instill excitement in others. The other side of the moon is the James Bond type—unflappable, stable, calculating. It's the unarousable investor who deals best with highly uncertain types of investments.

The last step of the analysis is to determine if you are a dominant or submissive person. Are you the hands-on type of investor? Would you consider yourself strong, fearless, relaxed in the face of danger? If one of your faults is interrupting the speech of others or being bossy, consider yourself dominant. If others think you are shy, unassuming, polite, it's a sign you are submissive by nature.

As you would expect, there is a wide array of degrees within the bounds of these three basic characteristic classifications. To deal with this, Dr. Mehrabian developed the following eight categories of personalities.

1. Exuberant = pleasant, arousable, dominant
2. Dependent = pleasant, arousable, submissive
3. Relaxed = pleasant, unarousable, dominant

4. Docile = pleasant, unarousable, submissive
5. Hostile = unpleasant, arousable, dominant
6. Anxious = unpleasant, arousable, submissive
7. Disdainful = unpleasant, unarousable, dominant
8. Bored = unpleasant, unarousable, submissive

Anyone interested in futures trading in any way, shape, or form falls into groups one through four. There is too much volatility and talk of risk to suit anyone in classifications five to eight.

Investors who trade for their own accounts and invest in new traders are usually found in Group Three. They are optimistic, can handle the ups and downs of the market, and want to take charge or help direct their trader.

People who prefer managed futures programs where they are removed from any direct participation tend to be in Group Four. They expect good things to happen, yet they are content to leave the actual trading up to someone else. The closer a Group Four investor leans toward Group Five, the more he or she would prefer a limited partnership or other type of program that defines the risk.

Dr. Mehrabian has written an excellent book that belongs on most investors' bookshelves. We've only been able to cover it briefly, so you may want to spend more time with it, particularly if you are not sure where you fit.

Let's concentrate for a while on what it takes to be a successful CTA. As we've just discussed, it helps to be of the Group Three persuasion from the psychological point of view.

But there is a lot more. To our way of thinking, a successful trader needs an edge on the market. Somehow trading success depends on outsmarting the hard psychology that dominates all markets—stocks, bonds, futures, cash, real estate.

If you think about the way classic bull markets develop, you can begin to get an insight into what an edge is. Bull markets are spawned by excess supply of the commodity in question. It might be too much money, corn, oil, or gold. The plentiful supply of this commodity encourages usage, and creative people find new uses for it.

As demand builds, prices start to inch higher. This gets the attention of inventory managers. Back when supplies were plentiful, they bought hand-to-mouth, no need to stockpile. If the price will be higher tomorrow, it pays to buy today. The activity of the inventory managers further stimulates prices. The pace of price increases picks up.

The trade press within the industry where the commodity is important fans the fires of demand. Insiders begin to speculate. Word spreads to the financial community and press quickly. Sooner or later, the mass media carries a story. That's when the average investor bids for a piece of the action, which usually signals a blow-off top. Prices crash.

At several points along the rocky road from bust to boom and back again, excellent trading opportunities present themselves. A technical trader watching a flat or stagnant price chart notices a slight uptrend. Perhaps the long-term downtrend line drawn earlier on the chart was penetrated. Or it might be a fundamental trader with informed contacts within the industry in question who hears talk of shortages, sees inventories decline, or notices price movements. This stimulates him or her to call some distributors, check import-export data, shipments, etc.—all the links in the chain from production to end use.

In either case, these traders get an edge on the herd. They begin with a few test trades. Is this a real change in trend or just a blip on the radar screen? If it is for real, they may pyramid their position by buying more and more positions with the unrealized gains from the earlier ones. This substantially increases leverage, profit potential, and risk. With a little luck, they exit before the blow-off top, using the story on the "Nightly News" as a signal.

Some of the best research into the anatomy of stock and futures traders was done by Jack D. Schwager and recorded in his two very readable books, *Market Wizards: Interviews with Top Traders* and *The New Market Wizards: Conversations with America's Top Traders*. Use these books to get an insight into how the great traders think, before you actually talk to any CTAs.

What you want to learn is what your prospective trader thinks is his or her edge. From what unique perspective do they view the action in the pits, which gives them an advantage over everyone else? A few examples from the *Wizard* books help illustrate the point.

- Linda Bradford Raschke was trained as a musician. She sees price patterns as refrains that repeat at intervals, often with a variation.

- Mark and Joe Ritchie, whose firm CRT has earned an estimated $1 billion in trading profits, credit the quality and team spirit of their employees.

- Monroe Trout, a legendary trader known for consistency and low drawdowns, believes his excellent timing stems from the computerized trading systems combined with his personal touch.

- Al Weiss is the personification of the long-term trend analysts, using charts that go back over 150 years.

- Jeff Yass applies mathematical game theory to options trading.

These are just a few of the world-renowned stock and futures traders interviewed. Mr. Schwager also spoke with Bruce Kovner, Richard Dennis, Paul Tudor Jones, William O'Neil, David Ryan, Mark Weinstein, and several others. You even get interviews with psychologists, like Charles Faulkner and Dr. Van K. Tharp, who specialize in studying achievers and solving psychological trading blocks.

Use these interviews to develop lists of questions to ask of the CTAs or traders you interview. You want to learn about their philosophy of dealing with winning and losing streaks and how much respect they have for the market.

Great traders tend to take what the market gives. They are confident, but humble. Anyone who tries to muscle or bully the market doesn't last long. All of the wizards were brought to their knees at one time or another in their trading careers. Recovering and learning from the experience separates the haves from the have nots.

There are no right or wrong answers to these questions, as there is no wrong or perfect way to trade the market. The key to success is not a magic trading system, but the person behind the system.

Nevertheless, there are certain native skills and behavior patterns that seem to be present in the majority of successful traders. Your antennae must be continuously sweeping to detect them as you mix it up within the futures industry.

The most important characteristic is desire, which most commonly manifests itself as a passion for the markets. These people follow the market constantly. They have quotation equipment everywhere—at the office and at home and a handheld system for in-between times. They rarely get tired of reading or talking about the markets.

Probably the second most important trait is discipline. Discipline to follow their trading system religiously, no matter what it is. Discipline to do the hard, dull work often required to keep up with the markets they trade. Discipline to adhere to their money management rules.

After these two, it is the willingness to put in hundreds of hours each month—whatever is necessary. Some markets trade 24 hours a day. It seems that you never get a break. These people read, read, read . . . study, study, study . . . trade, trade, trade.

There are even a few more mundane traits that also seem to be always present. One is above-average math skills. The market moves so fast sometimes and there is so much at stake, if you can't add, subtract, and multiply in 16ths, 32nds, and 64ths, you're going to make a serious error at some point. It helps to be able to instantaneously calculate a spread, straddle, or strangle in your head.

Successful traders have a prodigious memory for what appears to be minutiae concerning the markets they trade. Answers to questions like when and what was the last low for the October T-bond contract, pops to their mind like Babe Ruth's home run record. Chart pattern reliability, cycles, seasonal patterns, export figures, rainfall by month by county in Iowa, hog-corn ratios—the list of facts and figures goes on and on, depending on what they trade.

In your search for the perfect CTA—the next Paul Tudor Jones or Richard Dennis—develop a profile of what that person might be like. Then spend the time it takes to get to know that person as intimately as possible, since an awful lot can be riding on your interview.

12

Integrating Managed Futures
into Mainstream Portfolios

An enormous amount of research has been conducted over the years by well-known academics, as well as futures industry professionals, to determine the place of professionally managed futures in an investor's portfolio. Much of the best research has been collected in a single volume by Carl C. Peter. Serious students of the theories behind investment portfolio construction may want a copy of *Managed Futures: Performance, Evaluations, and Analysis of Commodity Funds, Pools, and Accounts* (Probus Publishing Company, 1992). It includes the work of scholars such as John Litner (Harvard), Scott H. Irwin (Ohio State University), Morton S. Baratz (*Managed Account Report*), and many others.

Much of the research deals with two important questions. First, is managed futures a good investment? And what impact will it have on an existing portfolio of stocks, bonds, and other assets? The Barclay Trading Group has updated much of the research done by these pioneering researchers to confirm that the results are still valid, despite market changes.

Barclay felt that some of the studies should be rerun using as current data as available because many of the older studies go back decades. Every day the markets trade, the results will vary even if it is ever so slightly. The critical issue is whether the general relationship between the alternative investment classes (stocks, bonds, cash, real estate, futures, etc.) remains the same. You also want the relationship between the asset classes and major economic factors, like inflation, to be constant. If they are, investors can make intermediate and long-range decisions based on the studies. New factors, like giant CTAs trading thousands of contracts per day and program trading on the stock exchanges, must be tested.

One way to quantify the positive or negative impact on an investor is to study managed futures in a variety of settings. We've studied managed futures in isolation, as the only investment in an investor's portfolio, and in combination with other asset classes.

As a stand-alone investment, managed futures has some pluses and minuses (see Exhibit 12.1). You'll see that the Barclay Index leads them in return and is fifth in the risk category. These figures cover the decade of the 1980s. Whenever you see information like this, try and put it in perspective. What were interest rates doing? Inflation? Was it a period of expansion or deflation? You need to do this because all investments do better or worse given certain economic conditions.

The positive aspect, of course, is the annual return figure of 19.8 percent; the negative is the risk figure at 14.6 percent, the fifth highest. Risk was measured as standard deviation from the mean, which we've already discussed. In other words, the results of the CTAs on the Barclay Index can be expected to fall within a range of approximately 15 percent of either side of the average annual return two-thirds of the time. This equates to a range of 30 percent and there is still approximately one-third that would be outside that range.

The stock market, as measured by the S&P 500, during this same period of time had a total range of about 25 percent, somewhat more stable than the CTA Index, while small stocks (lower capitalization) were actually more fickle, with a range of 36 percent. Once again,

EXHIBIT 12.1

10-Year Comparison of Risk and Return

	Annual Return	Risk
Barclay Index	19.8%	14.6% (5)
S&P 500	13.9%	12.6% (7)
U.S. Government Bonds	13.7%	13.4% (6)
Art	13.0%	14.9% (4)
Commercial Paper	9.4%	2.7% (9)
Small Stocks	9.3%	18.0% (1)
Commercial Real Estate	8.8%	4.3% (8)
T-Bills	8.5%	2.5% (10)
Inflation	4.5%	1.9% (11)
Residential Housing	4.4%	1.6% (12)
Gold	−1.9%	15.2% (3)
Venture Capital	−2.4%	17.9% (2)

Source: Barron's, Morgan Stanley, Barclay CTA Database.

NOTE: Ten-year performance comparison is for the period January 1981 through December 1990.

Risk is defined as the standard deviation of the annual returns.

these figures cover a specific time, the 10-year period ending December 1990.

The question any investor must ask is whether he or she would want their entire portfolio in a single asset group as temperamental as these. If not, what does one do to reduce volatility?

Before we get into a discussion of dividing or allocating assets among different asset classes to reduce volatility, we need to point out that the risk factor of the Barclay CTA Index is a composite figure of all the CTAs included in the index. This means that some of the CTAs are substantially more unpredictable and others more stable than the 14.6 percent standard deviation.

There is always the possibility that an investor could seek out one, two, or more CTAs that have very low volatility. Or, if they are volatile, they are erratic only on the positive side. Rather than putting all the eggs in one or two baskets, an investor might consider investing in several CTAs.

A Random Walk down LaSalle Street

In his investment classic *A Random Walk Down Wall Street*, Burton Malkiel explored the effects of combining different types of stocks into diversified stock portfolios. Building upon the earlier work of other leaders in the field of modern portfolio theory—such as Markowitz, Solnik, and Modigliani—Professor Malkiel made a number of important observations about the risk inherent in stock price movement.

In particular, he observed that an individual stock contains two elements of risk. The first type of risk is called systematic risk (also called market risk) and reflects the tendency of a stock to react to general swings in the stock market as a whole. The degree of the reaction to a market swing by a particular stock is measured by the Greek letter *beta*. The higher a stock's beta, the greater the tendency for the stock's price to move relative to a total market move.

The second element of risk reflected in the movement of a stock price is called *unsystematic risk,* and it results from factors that are specific to that particular stock. For example, the resignation of John Sculley as chairman of Apple Computer reflected an unsystematic risk factor specific to Apple Computer; whereas the stock market's decline on October 19, 1987, represented a systematic risk for the entire market.

Professor Malkiel also observed that by combining groups of randomly selected stocks, the unsystematic risk of a total stock portfolio could be reduced. In fact, in one of his most important findings he stated the following: "As the number of total securities in the portfolio approached 20, the total risk of the portfolio was reduced to the systematic level. All of the unsystematic risk had been eliminated. . . . That means that the unsystematic risk has essentially been washed away: An unexpected weather calamity is balanced by a favorable exchange rate, and so on. What remains is only the systematic risk of each stock in the portfolio, which is given by its beta." Malkiel's work, which was originally done in 1973, was reexamined following the Crash of '87 in the book's new 1990 edition and was found to be just as accurate today as it was then.

The Connection to Managed Futures

All this may be very interesting to a stock trader, but what is the connection to managed futures? After all, there is no such thing as unsystematic risk when it comes to measuring CTA performance. Or is there?

In an attempt to answer that question, we again called on the researchers at Barclay Trading Group. They decided to replicate Malkiel's classic study, but rather than combine individual stocks, they randomly combined the historical performance of groups of CTAs chosen from a universe of 25 CTAs. This universe included only CTAs having at least five years' performance history and was chosen on a pro rata weighted basis from each of the seven Barclay subindex categories to reflect the overall composition of the total CTA universe. (See Exhibit 12.2 for categories.)

In order to compare the effects of combining these CTAs in various portfolios versus investing with their individual performance results, they first examined individual performance results. Exhibit 12.3 is a scattergram that compares the compound annual return (the reward) for each CTA against the standard deviation of each CTA's monthly returns (the risk, or volatility). Each dot represents the return/risk profile of one CTA for the five-year period ending June 30, 1993.

The solid horizontal line in the scattergram indicates the average compound annual return for the group of 25 CTAs, which was 16.68 percent. The solid vertical line indicates the average monthly

EXHIBIT 12.2

CTA Category	No. of CTAs
Currency only	2
Agricultural only	1
Diversified	6
Energy only	1
Financials/Metals	4
Discretionary	4
Systematic	7
Total No. of CTAs in Sample Universe	25

Source: Barclay Trading Group, Ltd., Fairfield, IA.

standard deviation, which was plus or minus 6.45 percent. If an investor could pick an ideal location on the chart, then the obvious choice would be the upper left quadrant—high reward with low risk.

In the real world of investments, however, reward is almost always correlated with risk. In simplest terms, the higher the potential reward, the greater the risk that must be assumed in order to achieve that reward.

Managed futures is no exception to this universal investment rule. Evidence of this fact is provided by the sloping line in the scattergram. This line indicates the trend (i.e., the sum of least squares) of the reward/risk profiles of the 25 CTAs in the sample population. The trend line intersects the Y-axis (i.e., the point of zero risk) at approximately +6 percent. It is significant to note that 6 percent was just slightly more than the average risk-free rate during the five-year period of the study.

As can be readily seen, the performance results of each individual CTA are not neatly arrayed upon the trend line. In fact, some CTAs have had performances that deviate significantly from the

EXHIBIT 12.3

Reward/Risk Comparison for 25 CTAs

for the 5-year period ending 6/30/93

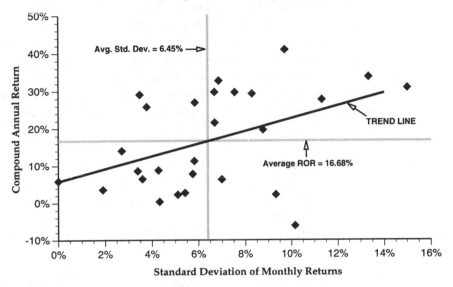

Source: Barclay Trading Group, Ltd., Fairfield, IA.

trend line. If one were to make a value judgment, the "superior" CTAs would be those whose profiles fall above the trend, and the inferior CTAs are those who fall below. Given the competitive nature of the managed futures industry, those CTAs above the trend line will likely succeed in raising large sums of investment capital, while those below may experience difficulty in surviving.

Another useful application of the scattergram is to compare the relative leverage applied to various CTAs. If an imaginary line is drawn perpendicular to the midpoint of the trend line, in general CTAs to the left of the line can be assumed to use relatively low amounts of leverage, while those to the right are probably more aggressive.

The Effects of Random Diversification

Having seen how the individual CTAs compared with each other in terms of reward and risk, Barclay next set out to randomly combine these 25 CTAs in portfolios of various sizes. The random CTA groupings ranged in size from only one CTA per portfolio (of which there were 25 possible portfolios), up to 25 CTAs per portfolio (only one possible portfolio). Perhaps 25 seems like a small universe to work with, but analyzing all possible combinations of 12 CTAs, for example, out of a total universe of 25 CTAs involves examining a total of 5,200,300 possible combinations. In all Barclay examined—or rather, their computer examined—a total of 33,554,431 portfolio combinations.

The results are presented in Exhibit 12.4. The solid line indicates the mean risk (as measured by standard deviation of monthly returns) for portfolios of increasing size. The dotted lines indicate plus or minus one standard deviation of risk for each portfolio size. In simplest terms, two-thirds of all portfolio risk levels fall between the dotted lines.

As we have already seen in the scattergram, the average risk for single-CTA portfolios was 6.45 percent, with a standard deviation of +/−2.80 percent. Thus, two-thirds of all single-advisor portfolios had risk levels between 3.65 percent and 9.25 percent.

By increasing the portfolio size from one to two CTAs, the average risk fell to 5.19 percent, about a 20 percent decrease in volatility. As can be seen in Exhibit 12.4, the decrease in risk becomes smaller with the addition of each new CTA to a portfolio. In fact, increasing the portfolio size from eight to nine CTAs reduces the average risk from 3.96 percent to 3.91 percent, an almost negligible decrease of only 0.05 percent. By the time we have 10 CTAs in a portfolio, the curve is virtually flat.

LaSalle Street Compared to Wall Street

Remember that Malkiel found that by randomly combining 20 stocks, a portfolio's unsystematic risk could be eliminated and only

EXHIBIT 12.4
Effects of Random Diversification
Portfolio Risk vs. Size of Portfolio

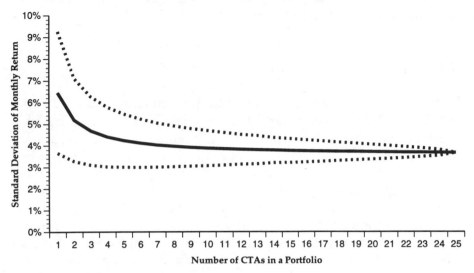

Source: Barclay Trading Group, Ltd., Fairfield, IA.

the systematic risk remained. Barclay's study indicates that by combining approximately 10 or fewer CTAs, the risk specific to individual CTA trading systems can be eliminated. What remains is the risk or volatility inherent in the futures markets in general.

This finding gives rise to an important question: Why is it that as few as 10 CTAs in a portfolio can eliminate the CTA-specific risk, while a stock portfolio requires 20 stocks to eliminate the unsystematic risk? The answer lies in the higher level of intracorrelation between individual stocks as compared to the average correlation between CTAs. Studies of individual stock correlation have indicated that the average correlation factor among all stocks is greater than +0.65. This means that even stocks with a high degree of unsystematic risk and a relatively high beta still have a strong tendency to move in tandem with the universe of stocks as a whole.

By comparison, in a prior study, Barclay Trading Group found that the average correlation factor among all CTAs was approximately +0.35. This difference is not surprising when one considers the variety of markets, trading systems, and investment holding periods favored by different CTAs.

Random versus Selective Diversification

Keep in mind that the study examined the results of random diversification, and these results represent the average risk for all possible portfolios as measured by computer simulation. Needless to say, this is not the process utilized by experienced trading managers when constructing a diversified managed futures portfolio. Obviously, only a small percentage of the total universe of all possible portfolio combinations would ever be seriously considered for investment.

Rather than randomly combining CTAs, an experienced trading manager selectively combines CTAs who are diverse in terms of trading methodology, market concentration, and average term of investment (i.e., short-term versus long-term). The trading manager will also utilize mathematical analysis to combine CTAs whose prior trading results have had a low degree of correlation.

By selectively combining noncorrelated CTAs in a portfolio, a smaller number of CTAs can provide a much greater reduction in risk than a similar number of randomly combined CTAs. In order to illustrate this point, Barclay intentionally combined a group of five diverse CTAs from the original sample universe of 25 CTAs. The average intercorrelation among the five selected CTAs was +0.14, a relatively low level of correlation.

Each of the five CTAs taken individually had a standard deviation of monthly returns between 5.82 percent and 6.69 percent. The average standard deviation for the group of five CTAs was 6.38 percent. However, when the five were combined into one portfolio, the portfolio as a whole had a standard deviation of 3.46 percent. As one would expect, the portfolio provides lower risk than any of the CTAs taken individually or than a randomly selected group of the same size.

Implications for the Investor

It is important to note that all of this research is based on historical CTA performance results. If historical volatility patterns by individual CTAs had little or no relationship to the CTA's future risk levels, then this research would be of limited value.

Fortunately, that appears not to be the case. Studies by Irwin, Ward, and Zulauf (1992, Appendix B) and others have found that whereas a CTA's future rates of return may have little correlation to his or her past performance, volatility levels among CTAs appear to have a relatively high degree of predictability. In other words, CTAs who have had low volatility levels in the past may reasonably be expected to maintain low volatility in the future. This is logical given the fact that certain CTAs use relatively low degrees of leverage, apply tight stop-limits, and do not concentrate their trading in a few positions; whereas other CTAs may trade much more aggressively by each of those parameters.

The implication for the investor is that a well-constructed multi-advisor portfolio of CTAs may perform a function similar to a mutual fund. The overall risk may be significantly reduced, while at the same time the portfolio may have the opportunity to participate in a variety of markets using a variety of trading styles. The trade-off when compared to a single-advisor approach is that the opportunity for exceptionally high rates of return during certain periods may be diminished. For the serious investor, however, a multi-advisor portfolio that is selectively diversified may provide the best long-term results, both in terms of reward and risk.

We asked Barclay to take this thought process one step further. What happens if managed futures and stocks are combined? They used the S&P 500 to represent a stock portfolio and the Barclay CTA Index for the futures portion. Successful diversification requires more than simply "spreading the risk." In fact, true success requires that two important conditions be met:

- The various portfolio components should have a relatively low correlation with each other.
- Each component should be profitable in and of itself over extended periods of time.

This second point leads to an interesting misconception regarding the concept of correlation. The misconception goes something like this: "If two investments have a negative correlation—i.e., they have an inverse relationship—then over the long run the returns from these two investments cancel each other out."

This is not the case. In fact, the performance of the U.S. stock market compared to the managed futures industry provides a striking example. For the five-year period ending December 31, 1991, the S&P 500 Total Return Index advanced approximately 103.9 percent, for a compound annual return of 15.32 percent. During the same five-year period the Barclay CTA Index advanced 146.2 percent, for a compound annual return of 19.74 percent.

Although both the S&P 500 and the Barclay CTA Index were profitable, the paths they took to profitability were very different. For example, Exhibit 12.5 shows the monthly returns for the Barclay CTA Index and the S&P 500 for a 36-month span. Even a cursory examination reveals that managed futures and stocks tended to perform differently during specific periods of time.

As Exhibit 12.6 shows, during 24 of the 36 months, managed futures and stocks tended to move in opposite directions—i.e., one posted a gaining month while the other posted a loss. During nine months, both stocks and managed futures posted a gain. Only three times during the 36-month period did both stocks and managed futures show a loss during the same month.

Similar results can be seen over the 60 months. Stocks and managed futures moved in opposite directions 60 percent of the time. Both showed gains approximately 30 percent of the time, while both had negative returns only about 8 percent of the time.

EXHIBIT 12.5

Comparison of Monthly Returns

Barclay CTA Index vs. S&P 500, Jan. '91–Dec. '93

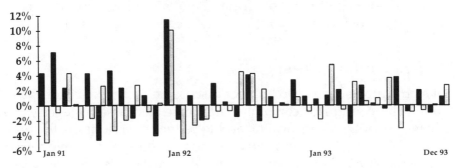

Source: Barclay Trading Group, Ltd., Fairfield, IA.

EXHIBIT 12.6

Monthly Returns of Barclay CTA Index and S&P 500

for Periods Ending 12/31/91

Time Period	Opposite	Both Positive	Both Negative
Past 36 mos.	24 Mos.	9 Mos.	3 Mos.
% Occurrence	66.7%	25.0%	8.3%
Past 60 Mos.	36 Mos.	19 Mos.	5 Mos.
% Occurrence	60.0%	31.7%	8.3%

Source: Barclay Trading Group, Ltd., Fairfield, IA.

This recent history demonstrates how two dissimilar investments can both achieve profitability over an extended period of time in a noncorrelated fashion. The net result of a portfolio diversified across these two investments during these five years would have been a smoothing of the growth curve and a reduction in the portfolio's overall volatility.

Modern Portfolio Theory

Let's now move to an even broader discussion of the subject of correlation. The concept of combining noncorrelated asset categories to achieve portfolio diversification and to reduce overall risk is the bedrock of Modern Portfolio Theory. Although some critics have raised questions about the implementation of modern portfolio theory— e.g., exactly how do you define what a noncorrelated asset is—few argue with the overall logic that sound diversification reduces the risk of a catastrophic loss.

With regard to managed futures, much has been written about its role as a value-added portfolio component. The consensus among most analysts is that managed futures as a class tends to perform in a manner that is uncorrelated with the traditional asset classes of stocks and bonds.

Less has been written about the fact that domestic equity and fixed-income instruments have generally become more positively correlated in recent years. As a result, the need for an "alternative asset" category is greater today than it was 30 years ago. The classic "60/40" stock and bond portfolio may no longer provide the diversification it once did.

The accuracy of both these assertions will be examined, with the help of Barclay Trading Group's research, in light of recent performance trends. Rather than simply observe these phenomena of correlation and noncorrelation, Barclay will also investigate the underlying causal relationships. Too often, noncorrelation is measured in quantitative terms only, without regard to understanding why such relationships exist. In our opinion, if the reasons for correlation or noncorrelation between two events cannot be identified, it's a risky proposition to assume that such a relationship will continue to exist in the future.

Correlation, as mentioned earlier, is often misunderstood to mean that two positively correlated investments will perform exactly alike. Conversely, it's also falsely assumed that negatively correlated investments cancel each other out. The reality of correlation analysis is more complex.

The degree of intercorrelation between two investments can be defined quantitatively by measuring the historical tendency of the two investments to move in the same or opposite directions relative to their average gain/loss during the same periods of time. Correlation measurement depends upon two factors: (1) the direction, and (2) the magnitude of a periodic performance result relative to that investment's mean periodic performance result.

The range of possible correlation coefficients is from +1.0 to –1.0. A correlation coefficient of +1.0 indicates a perfect positive correlation—i.e., the tendency to move in the same direction and same magnitude relative to the mean at the same time. A correlation coefficient of –1.0 indicates an inverse relationship—i.e., the tendency to move in opposite directions relative to the mean at the same time. A correlation coefficient of 0 indicates a random or neutral relationship.

Crude oil and gasoline provide an example of two commodities that have a high positive correlation. If the price of crude oil has increased significantly, it's a very safe bet that gasoline prices have also gone up. On the other hand, the price of bonds and the T-bill rate provide an example of negative correlation. If the T-bill rate has declined, it's very likely that bond prices will have increased. Neutral correlation can be demonstrated by comparing two unrelated commodities such as Japanese silk and pork bellies. If the price of silk has plummeted, that doesn't necessarily convey any useful information regarding the price of pork bellies.

A Look at Recent Correlation Trends

Exhibits 12.7, 12.8, and 12.9 chart the recent correlation trends among stocks, bonds, and managed futures. Stock market performance is measured by monthly returns of the S&P 500 Total Return Index (including reinvestment of dividends). Bond market performance is measured by the monthly returns of the Lehman Long-Term Bond Index (which includes reinvestment of interest). Finally, managed futures performance is measured by the Barclay CTA Index.

In each case, correlation has been measured on a rolling 36-month-period basis. This means that each data point on the charts represents the correlation for the prior 36 months.

Exhibit 12.7 demonstrates the correlation of managed futures versus stocks since December 1982. The highest correlation between stocks and managed futures was +0.33. This occurred in September 1987, just prior to the crash. The lowest correlation was –0.32, which occurred in October 1991.

Exhibit 12.8 shows the correlation between managed futures and bonds. The overall pattern is similar to that of managed futures versus stocks. Although the most recent relationship is positive, the trend from 1987 to 1992 has been toward lower correlation. In 1993, it

EXHIBIT 12.7

Correlation of Barclay CTA Index vs. S&P 500

Rolling 36-Month Time Periods, 1982–1993

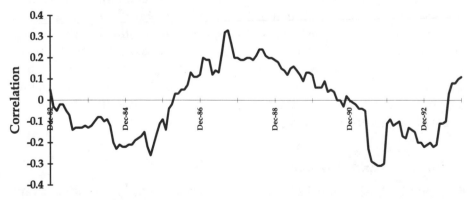

Source: Barclay Trading Group, Ltd., Fairfield, IA.

EXHIBIT 12.8

Correlation of Barclay CTA Index vs. Long-Term Bonds

Rolling 36-Month Time Periods, 1982–1993

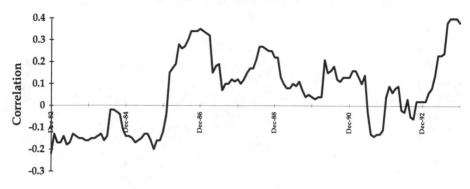

Source: Barclay Trading Group, Ltd., Fairfield, IA.

hit new highs due to the low interest rates and high bond prices, which aren't expected to be permanent.

Exhibit 12.9, however, presents a different relationship. Stocks and bonds have had a positive correlation for the entire 10-year period, except for a brief 3-month period in 1989 when the correlation was neutral. The recent trend has been toward a more positive correlation, with the highest correlation occurring in November 1992 (+0.66).

The overall intercorrelation among stocks, bonds, managed futures, and European stocks over the past 13 years is indicated in Exhibit 12.10. European stocks are measured by the monthly performance of the Morgan Stanley EAFE Index. As the table demonstrates, managed futures have had a virtually neutral correlation with each of the other three traditional investment sectors. The average intercorrelation among the other three, however, was +0.34, indicating a fairly high level of positive correlation.

EXHIBIT 12.9

Correlation of S&P 500 vs. Long-Term Bonds

Rolling 36-Month Time Periods for Jan. 1, 1982–April 30, 1993

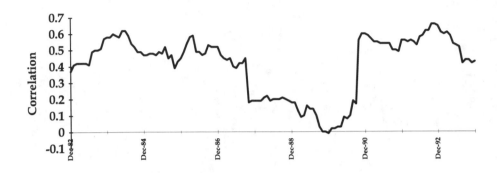

Source: Barclay Trading Group, Ltd., Fairfield, IA.

A Long-Term View of Stock and Bond Correlation

The recent tendency of stocks and bonds to have a high positive correlation is no short-term aberration. In fact, this trend toward a more positive correlation has existed for many years. Using data derived from Ibbotson and Sinquefield, Barclay found that during the 1950s and 1960s the overall correlation between stocks and bonds was approximately neutral.

For example, during the '50s, the correlation between stocks and bonds (measured on a rolling five-year basis) ranged between –0.30 and +0.35. During the '60s the range became slightly more positive (–0.28 to +0.50). But during the '70s and '80s, the relationship was entirely positive (+0.20 to +0.60) and during the '90s the positive correlation has increased even further.

EXHIBIT 12.10

Intercorrelations of Major Indices

January 1, 1980–April 30, 1993

	Barclay CTA Index	S&P 500 Total Return Index	Lehman Brothers Bond Index	Morgan Stanley EAFE Index
Barclay CTA Index	1.00	0.05	−0.02	−0.02
S&P 500 Total Return Index	0.05	1.00	0.34	0.45
Lehman Brothers Bond Index	−0.02	0.34	1.00	0.23
Morgan Stanley EAFE Index	−0.02	0.45	0.23	1.00

Source: Barclay Trading Group, Ltd., Fairfield, IA.

What's Behind the Numbers

Many astute investors are not fully aware of the fact of increasing stock/bond correlation or its implications for portfolio construction. Also, among those who are aware of this phenomenon, there is a variety of opinions as to why this is occurring. There are several factors involved.

Chief among them is the increased interest rate volatility experienced over the past 10 years, which may have caused a stronger positive relationship between stock trading and interest rate moves. This, in turn, translates into a higher correlation between stock and bond movements. For example, an increase in domestic interest rates or an upsurge in inflation would have a negative effect on both stock and bond prices.

The noncorrelation of managed futures with stocks and bonds is less difficult to understand. First, CTAs are able to easily trade the financial markets from both long and short sides and profit from declining as well as gaining trends. By contrast, very few investors in the stock market short it.

Second, an event that creates economic uncertainty and puts pressure on the traditional sectors usually presents profitable trading opportunities to CTAs. The invasion of Kuwait by Iraq was one such event. During the onset of the Gulf crisis, from July through October 1990, the S&P 500 declined 14.11 percent while the Barclay CTA Index increased 17.70 percent. CTAs were able to profit from trends in the energy complex and other physical commodities and the downward trend in the financial complex.

Monthly returns for stocks and managed futures have moved in opposite directions in approximately 57 percent of all months during the past 10 years. The two were both positive in 31 percent of all months, and both negative in only 12 percent of the monthly periods.

The theoretical arguments favoring the noncorrelation of managed futures versus stocks and bonds are compelling. More importantly, the experience of the past 10 years corroborates the theory.

An obvious point that is worth noting, however, is that noncorrelation is not the only factor that justifies inclusion of managed futures in a portfolio. The other critical factor is that the alternative investment category must be profitable in its own right. As one observer stated: "Who needs noncorrelation if it will lose money?"

Further investigation shows that managed futures holds its own on the return issue as well. Since January 1, 1980, the Barclay CTA Index has had a compound annual return of 19.56 percent (through April 30, 1993) versus 15.55 percent for the S&P 500 and 12.46 percent for the Lehman Bond Index.

Even during one of the strongest bull markets in the history of the stock market, managed futures has emerged as a viable diversification element for the serious portfolio manager. The potential benefits could be even greater if the stock market reverts to its long-term 65-year average gain of 12.5 percent per year.

13

Where Do You Look for the Next Paul Tudor Jones?

For the uninitiated, Paul Tudor Jones has had, and is still having, a spectacular career as a futures trader. If you had invested $1,000 in the Tudor Future Fund at its inception in September 1984, you would have had $17,482 by October of 1988. He combined five consecutive years in a row of triple-digit annual returns. During the month no one on Wall Street forgets, October 1987, his fund registered a 62 percent gain.

Unfortunately, he is no longer accepting money. As a matter of fact, he's making distributions. This is one of the important "catch 22s" of the managed futures industry. Once a money manager becomes famous, he or she is no longer accessible because his or her minimum investment is out of the reach of everyone but the largest investors. If the CTA is not famous, there is probably a good reason—untested or weak stats.

What happens in managed money is not unlike what happens in any high stakes, competitive undertaking, or sport. If there is skill and luck involved, all the money flows to the superstars. Equity pours down the sieve from the many to the few that outperform all others. At some point, the few become overloaded. Excess venture capital must search for new talent. Great new traders enter the competition and work their way to the top.

The big question is where do you find people with the talent to become trading titans. As my granddad used to say: "If you're looking for a cowboy, you need to be somewhere you can smell horse manure." One of the first places to start sniffing around is the commodity exchanges. People who have the desire, risk tolerance, and confidence are drawn to LaSalle and Jackson streets like starlets are to Hollywood and Vine.

There are a variety of entry-level positions available that facilitate breaking into the industry. The most common is to become a runner. They carry orders between the telephone order desks at the exchanges and the floor traders. The next step up is working the order desk itself. With a little luck, some of these people become assistants to a floor trader, who teaches them the business.

Because of the high cost of buying or leasing a seat on an exchange, which is required to trade on the floor, many of the would-be CTAs gravitate to the outer fringes of the trading floor. It is very common for emerging CTAs to be found sharing space and price quotation equipment with other would-be superstars in crowded offices at or near the CBOT (Chicago Board of Trade), the Merc (Chicago Mercantile Exchange), or one of the New York futures exchanges. You can also find them in Kansas City and Minneapolis, but not in such a large variety as in Chicago.

To support themselves while waiting to be discovered, many function as brokers. They may work directly for an FCM (futures commission merchant), handling proprietary business, or they may deal with the public. As a rule, it is a very cliquish society. To crack it, you need to befriend a few of the insiders. This isn't difficult, since most of them are looking for new money to trade. Herein lies danger!

Most of the ones who will succeed have a flair for salesmanship or even showmanship. It is one thing to be a good trader. It's quite another to have the world recognize it. Therefore, you need to be able to penetrate the smoke and mirrors you'll encounter to separate the real ore from the fool's gold.

The analytic skills you've learned so far definitely give you an edge. The problem you'll run into is that most of these unacclaimed traders don't have a long enough track record to provide statistical reliability to your analysis. We like at least three years and preferably five.

Next, the trading record may be in a disorganized format—shoe boxes overflowing with statements for the last two years. Organizing it into something you can make sense out of may be a Herculean feat. Last of all, the amount of money being traded may not be sufficient to give you confidence in your analysis.

All along, this Richard Dennis look-alike (he's a legend in the commodity industry; read *Market Wizards*) is doing everything in his or her power to raise your greed level to a fever pitch. "Just give me $100,000 and three months to double or triple your money!" You'll learn how the one or two minor flaws in the system have been corrected and it is now ready to break the bank.

Time out for a reality check! Remember what was said about showmanship and selling. Charlatans and mountebanks flock to all actively traded markets in search of investors blinded by greed. The futures market is no different from the stock, real estate, or any other marketplace.

The investor who gets burned is the one who doesn't do his or her homework. Spend time with potential traders. Find out how strong their passion for the market is. What sacrifices have they made? You can often tell the real McCoy from the con man by visiting their office. If it's cluttered, filled with market data, that's a good sign. If the candidate is more interested in the markets during trading hours than you, that's another good sign. Interviews with their supervisor (virtually everyone who's an insider is registered with the NFA and would have a compliance supervisor) may provide some insight. An independent CTA would not have a direct supervisor, but would have to clear trades through someone. Don't forget the NFA Information Center.

You're looking for someone who is a serious student of the markets. A knowledgeable individual with a good reputation; someone with enough experience and intelligence to have a serious chance at stardom.

What if you're not near an exchange? You then tap into the network that feeds into the market, i.e., brokerage firms. Brokers generally work for independent Introducing Brokers (IBs) or branch offices of major firms. Some specialize in managed money. A few phone calls to local firms (try the Yellow Pages as a last resort) tells you if any can help.

If they can't, they'll attempt to talk you out of managed money by explaining all the disadvantages. You'll learn that it is expensive (high fees) and risky (what isn't?) and that you may have to tie your money up for long periods of time, a year or more. There is some truth to all this and we'll show you how to avoid most of these obstacles, but the point is that brokers who respond this way don't sell managed programs. Therefore, they can't help.

At the other end of the spectrum is the broker who knows every CTA in the world. Two days following your first call, you're inundated with a ton and a half of dis-docs and prospectuses. This group of brokers is indiscriminate in its selection and does little research.

Try to locate a broker somewhere in the middle. This person will spend time with you to learn what you're after. His or her firm will have a list of approved CTAs, or at least a list of ones they recommend—backed by research and analysis. They may have a CTA or two on staff who trades for their customers. Or they may have their own pool or limited partnership.

As mentioned earlier, many hopeful CTAs start as brokers. This is true all over the country, as well as in Chicago. The advantage of giving a broker discretion is that you can often test his or her ability utilizing a small amount of equity, sometimes less than $25,000.

The minimum account a CTA will accept can be a very limiting factor—limiting in the number of trading programs open to investors. As mentioned at the beginning of this chapter, some of the best traders are not accepting new accounts. Other established ones command high minimums: $100,000, $500,000, and even $1 million is not uncommon. The reason for requiring a half million or more is to qualify the investor as sophisticated and to be able to fully diversify the account. Thus the systematic risk in the account is neutralized.

Larger accounts also have a greater statistical chance of being successful. They can withstand some drawdown, yet still have enough equity available when market conditions are prime for the trading system. Profits in futures are generated by three rights—right market, right side of market (long or short), and right time. Deep pockets means staying power until all three rights line up in a row. The big CTAs know this and have the reputation to demand the high minimums.

Rather than a CTA, you might try a futures broker. The negative side of giving a broker limited power of attorney (discretion) to trade your account is the limited statistical data that's usually available. Your best play is to pick his or her brain as much as possible, in person or over the phone. Then try a very limited, controlled program for a short period of time, such as three months. Do not tell the broker there is a time limit. It puts undue pressure on him or her and makes him or her force some big trades before time runs out, which could result in serious loss. After one quarter, reevaluate. You may want to try three more months, or you may want to pick up your marbles and go home. To find the right broker, you may have to do this over and over and over.

As you get immersed in the futures industry, you learn many other ways of uncovering traders. (You can find the addresses and telephone numbers of the sources mentioned in this section in Appendix B.) One of the most commonly used is *Futures Magazine*. Each year it does a feature on hot new traders. The general qualification to be considered for this article is for the trading advisor to have a three-year track record and less than $10 million under management. *Futures* advertises for traders to submit their records. It then selects a half dozen or so for inclusion in the article. These advisors naturally are seeking attention and new money. You might also want to check out its classified section, where some CTAs advertise.

There are several other publications worth noting. *Managed Account Report*, mentioned earlier for its CTA indexes, has chronicled the managed money industry just about since its inception. Each issue of the *MAR* newsletter includes a "Trading Manager Review," which includes biographical information, as well as a complete summary of the trader's system and stats.

Commodity Trader Consumer Report newsletter tracks the trading system of a group of carefully selected CTAs each month. You can match your candidate(s) against the record of this group (some of these track records are hypothetical). Also, it includes interviews with the top CTAs and news about the industry.

Managed Futures Today: The Industry Forum is directed more to the industry insider. But sometimes it helps to know what is concerning the people who manage the area you're considering investing in. Another insider newsletter is *Managed Futures Information,* which reports on news about companies in the managed futures industry. These industry-type newsletters often talk about CTAs who are making news or innovating. They'll sometimes tip you off to a CTA to check out or an idea that's on the cutting edge.

The professionals within this industry have their own trade association, the Managed Futures Association. Its function is to assist members, to promote the industry, and to advance the industry. They produce an excellent monthly professional journal that discusses issues important to members, everything from legislation, regulatory compliance, trade execution, to marketing. Their annual membership directory is an excellent source to find CTAs and CPOs.

Commodity pool operators are the individuals or corporations who structure funds. These are pools of commingled money from a number of individual investors. Most of the funds are large enough to require multiple CTAs. If the funds are properly selected, this further reduces risk, as we saw earlier. Most CPOs closely follow the performance of a large number of CTAs and analyze their performance. For this reason, CPOs can be excellent consultants in CTA selection.

Besides the MFA Membership Directory, there are other industry directories available. *Futures Magazine* publishes an annual reference guide, which includes a section on CTAs and CPOs.

The NFA will provide, for a nominal fee, the names, addresses, and telephone numbers of all registrants by category, i.e., CTAs, CPOs, IBs, FCMs, etc. The only problem with the CTA list is you can't tell which ones are active. Someone could be registered as a CTA, but not actually trading. Christopher Resources Inc. puts out a similar list on computer diskette. This makes it easy to update and/or import into a database for future reference.

Speaking of databases, there are several available. Here's a list of the leading ones:

- Barclay Trading Group
- LaPorte Asset Allocation
- Prudential Securities Incorporated
- TASS Management Ltd.

Several of these databases include analytical software, allowing the license holder to run the numbers to his or her heart's content. Most offer a monthly update of each CTA's statistics. Some, like Prudential's, are proprietary and available only through their brokers or correspondent brokers. Barclay provides a quarterly hard copy update to subscribers.

Several of these database services, LaPorte for example, include the phrase "asset allocation." This means they consult with clients to blend managed futures programs with an investor's or institution's overall portfolio. Barclay Trading Group is another firm that consults in this area.

Other fertile areas to search for emerging CTAs are trade shows and trading contests. Some commodity firms attend what are generally called money shows, which are retail exhibitions covering a wide variety of investments. Twice a year the MAR conducts a conference on futures money management. At this meeting, you can find quite a few CTAs. Since this is an industry-type trade show, the CTAs are primarily interested in getting the attention of FCMs who have large numbers of brokers who can promote their program (if they can get on the FCM's approval list). The topics discussed are also of more interest to someone in the industry than to an investor. Nevertheless, it is a place to get exposure to CTAs.

What Suits Your Needs

Who are you? What are you looking for? What are your needs? How much can you invest? These questions must be answered in order to sort out the various sources for CTAs.

The best approach is to use some examples. If you are a small investor with $5,000 or so of risk capital to invest, consider a fund, pool, or limited partnership. We'll be talking about these in more detail, but the primary reasons to choose these are predefined and limited risk, plus it's the only way to get adequate diversification of CTAs and markets with $5,000.

The term "risk capital" is critical. It refers to money an investor has available to use to speculate. Another description is money that, if lost, will not alter the investor's lifestyle.

Only risk capital should be used for highly speculative investments, such as raw land, gas and oil exploration, and futures. The high risk is balanced by the potential for high return.

The investor with a solid portfolio of stocks, bonds, real estate, insurance, a retirement plan and $25,000 to $100,000 of risk capital has different needs. The objective for this person might be to boost the return of the overall portfolio by obtaining high returns from futures. A successful investment in futures can lift the normally modest return generated by the cash and/or bond portions of the portfolio. (See Exhibit 13.1.) An additional benefit, as we saw when we analyzed the correlation of futures to stocks, is reduced volatility.

This concept is the backbone of Modern Portfolio Theory developed by Harry Markowitz in the 1950s, as referenced earlier. The investor sorts through various allocations of his or her assets to find what is known as the efficient frontier (see Chapter 15 for an example). This is the best mixture of assets to generate the most return with the least amount of fluctuation or volatility. The allocation or reallocation process needs to be reviewed periodically, as economic

EXHIBIT 13.1

Use of a Managed Futures Account to Enhance Overall Portfolio Return

Total size of investment portfolio	$200,000
A 12% return on portfolio	24,000
Reallocation:	
$180,000 remains in investments generating 12%	21,600
$20,000 placed in managed futures acct. generating 35%	7,000
Total return	$28,600

Overall portfolio increases from 12% to 14.3%, or approximately 20%.

conditions change. Investments, for example, that do well during inflationary periods, like physical commodities, should be increased as the CPI rises and reduced as it falls.

There are several strategies for the investor with $25,000 to $100,000 allocated to managed futures. Much of his or her decision will be based on the amount of time to be devoted to the project. Working with an individual trader is a possibility, or investing in a managed program with a CTA. A search of one of the databases mentioned earlier could produce a list of CTAs with minimum investments of $25,000. Or you could contact a broker or a consultant for a list of recommended CTAs. By the way, the cost of acquiring and maintaining most of the databases is prohibitive for most individuals. It wouldn't be uncommon for a broker to have access to one at his or her firm if the firm promoted managed money. This size of investor might also include a fund or limited partnership as part of his or her managed futures portfolio—perhaps $5,000 on the $25,000 level and $25,000 on the $100,000 level. The objective is increased diversification.

As always, the larger the investor the more alternatives there are open. When we move to investors with $500,000 to $1 million or more, diversification strategies become even more flexible. Futures portfolios of these sizes should include a professional asset allocation specialist. Once risk-reward parameters were agreed upon by the investor, the trading advisor would run various optimization routines over a CTA database to select suitable candidates. The better databases can simulate the investor's entire investment portfolio and suggest a variety of ways of increasing returns and lowering volatility.

When we get to the large institutional investor, with tens or hundreds of millions of dollars allocated to managed futures, like the Virginia Retirement Program, the question is whether analysis and management should be done in-house or by consultants.

The size of these accounts creates entirely new challenges. A CTA trading ten lots, or contracts, of March T-bonds at a time is inconspicuous in the market. When he or she jumps to 100 or 500 lots, the floor traders begin to take notice. At 1,000 lots or larger, problems begin to arise. The CTA must divide large orders among brokers, exchanges, and trading sessions (some futures contracts have more than one trading session each day). The CTA worries about artificially moving market with very large orders because it may come back to haunt him. What impact do all these changes have on the trading system? Can it continue to perform as it has previously when so many adjustments must be made?

Whoever allocates the money to the CTAs must diversify by trading style as well as by commodities traded. And these must be deep, liquid markets to absorb the new money.

Once all the allocation is complete, the real work of monitoring begins. Balance is the key. The portfolio cannot become overweighted in any one commodity or specific contract. If necessary, adjustments must be made daily. Daily feedback from all CTAs is required and must be evaluated before the next trading day.

The MOM (manager of managers)—or the preferred term, "trading managers"—needs to eat, sleep, and drink with the CTAs. He or she must know how they are doing psychologically as well as on paper. Adjustments, because of personal or technical problems, should be addressed before they get out of control. Running a

$1 million or $5 million futures portfolio is like steering the USS *Iowa*. Its momentum carries it forward for a long time, even after the captain has said: "Hard to starboard!"

From the $5,000 to the $5 million portfolio, there is a proper blend of markets, traders, and advisors. It might be a broker helping a new investor get started or a major advisory service servicing a pension plan. The most important criterion is that the investor's needs be met.

A caveat—even if you discover the most perfect aspirant, you have no guarantee of success. Few, if any, world-class traders in any market always make money. Even a virtuoso like George Soros takes a hit now and then. We recommend that you do your due diligence, work hard to find the program(s) based on your needs, and diversify to remove as much systematic risk as possible.

CTA Due Diligence Checklist

1. Is he or she, and the investment program(s), in good standing and properly registered with federal and state regulators?

   ( ) SEC ( ) CFTC ( ) NASD ( ) NFA ( ) Seller's State ( ) Buyer's State

2. Have any customer complaints, law suits, or other disciplinary actions been taken against the CTA and/or the firm?

3. Does he or she have a good reputation within the investment community?

4. Has a disclosure document been provided? If so, is it satisfactory?

5. Does the registration history obtained from the NFA agree with what you've been told and with what is in the disclosure document?

6. Do the client references check out?

7. Is the fee structure in line with industry standards?

8. How does the trading performance compare to the Barclay and the MAR CTA Indexes?

9. Are the performance ratios acceptable?

10. Is the CTA well organized and properly staffed?

11. Did anything unusual or suspicious occur during the selling process, such as high-pressure sales tactics or a hypothetical track record represented as an actual one?

12. Were you allowed to make a careful study of the entire proposition and were you given plenty of time to make up your mind?

13. Were you provided all the documentation you requested?

14. Is there any reason to suspect that your investment would have any negative impact on the CTA's performance or cause any major change in the current trading practices?

Always keep in mind—If it seems too good to be true, it probably is!

14

Paperwork and Other Regulatory Matters

Your choice of investment vehicles ranges from an individual account with unlimited risk to funds that guarantee the return of your principal. There is also a wide assortment of legal procedures you can take if you feel you have been treated unfairly.

On the most basic level, you can open a futures trading account and give your broker authority to trade your account. The first step is filling out what are known as account papers. The most important of these documents include:

1. *Acknowledgment of Receipt of Risk Disclosure Statement*—By signing this, you acknowledge you understand everything that could go wrong in your trading account and that you accept these risks. Key among the risks are that you could lose more than your original investment, at times market conditions may be such that you cannot liquidate a losing trade (limit up or down days), placing protective stop loss orders will not necessarily control losses, spreads may not be less risky than straight long or short positions, and the

high degree of leverage in this investment can work against you, as well as for you.

2. *Disclosure Statement for Noncash Margin*—Cash in your account is held in a segregated account, which would be returned to you in the unlikely event of a bankruptcy of the brokerage firm. But with noncash margin, commonly held in T-bills in street name, you would only receive a prorated share after a bankruptcy. The bankruptcy court would recognize you as a general creditor for the amount you hold in noncash margin. On the brighter side, no customer has lost money to date due to a bankruptcy of a futures brokerage firm.

3. *Futures Account Client Agreement*—This details your rights and responsibilities as a client. Chief among them is to maintain the proper amount of margin money in your account to cover the contracts being traded. If you fall short, you receive a margin call. If that is not met promptly, the FCM can close out your positions. This could happen at an inopportune time.

4. *Personal and Financial Information*—You must provide an overview of your personal and financial situation so that the broker, his firm (IB), and the FCM can determine if you are suited to trade futures. The CFTC obligates them to do this, as the SEC does with stock investors.

5. *Consent to Check Credit*—You give them the right to have your credit reviewed.

6. *Authorization to Transfer Funds*—This allows the FCM to move money from one of your accounts, say a stock account, to another, like the futures, if needed and if you have more than one account. Transfers take place only within the firm you are opening an account with. They do not have the right to go to other accounts at other firms to transfer your money.

7. *Consent to Cross Trades*—This one simply means that the broker, IB, and FCM may be on opposite sides of trades you are

carrying. You may be long; they short. It is usually an optional form.

8. *Arbitration Agreement*—This one is always optional, by CFTC regulation. It binds you to arbitration by the NFA in case of a dispute and you give up the right to sue. NFA registrants, like brokers and CTAs, are always bound by NFA arbitration.

9. *Joint Account Agreement*—You acknowledge you are aware that if you open an account jointly with someone else, your joint tenant can bind you to trades that you can be held liable for. It is also specific whether the account is held as a joint tenancy or in common.

10. *Commodity Option Agreement*—This is an acknowledgment, similar to futures risk disclosures, that you understand and accept all the risks of options-on-futures trading. Most FCM require this, even if you do not plan to trade options.

11. *W-9*—A W-9 is needed for U.S. citizens so that the FCM knows what income tax account to charge profits or losses to at the end of the year. Otherwise, 20 percent of gains must be withheld when payouts are made to the owner of the account.

12. *Special Account Forms*—If the account was to be opened in the name of a corporation, a corporate resolution would be required. Commercial hedgers and partnerships call for additional forms. Your broker normally supplies any additional forms required.

All this paperwork is needed to open your account, but more is needed to give trading discretion to a third party. As mentioned earlier, a power of attorney (POA) must be executed. Most people use a limited power of attorney, allowing the trader only the right to enter and exit trades. A standard POA is available from most brokerage firms.

You're not done yet. A CTA is required to provide you with a current disclosure document, which we have already discussed. You must sign a form acknowledging you received one. This form is called Disclosure Document Confirmation (DDC).

What about your spouse's nephew who is not registered with the NFA or your broker who is? Part 2 of the DDC states that you were not provided a dis-doc and leaves space for an explanation. Your nephew, being a direct relative, is exempt. So is your broker, if taking discretion (DRT) in your account is incidental to his or her brokerage services and it is done for your convenience, not his or hers. Some CTAs are also exempt from the dis-doc requirement. These CTAs have fewer than 15 clients over a twelve-month period of time, manage small amounts of money, and do not hold themselves out to the public (sales, PR, advertising, etc.) as CTAs. In certain circumstances, one or more of the exchanges may ask for a release of some sort.

If your CTA is a mainstream professional, you additionally have to sign his or her paperwork, which is contained in the disclosure document. Basically, you acknowledge that you understand all the risks, the fee structure, the material facts about him or her, the trading system, and how your account will be traded. You'll also be asked to sign an agreement to allow the CTA's fees to be paid directly from your brokerage account. Remember that the CTA and the broker who introduced you to the CTA may not be at the same firm.

That wraps up the paperwork on an individual account. The key issue is that the risk and reward are usually greatest with this type of arrangement. Your CTA or broker (with trading discretion) can trade your account into debit. That's when more money is lost than is in the account. On the positive side, the reward can be the greatest because the fees on these types of accounts are usually the lowest. There are few middlemen, like CPOs, and minimum legal expenses. Savvy investors negotiate the incentive, management, and brokerage fees until the CTA yells uncle!

Direct Participation Programs

The next level up in size and complexity is direct participation programs, or DPPs. You may think of them as tax shelters or limited partnerships (LPs). They are constructed to pass through all of their income, gains, losses, and tax benefits to their owners. The partnership itself pays no taxes because the partners accept liability. Gas-oil exploration and real estate development are common LPs.

Unlike those big sisters, the commodity trading limited partnership is not a tax shelter. It is structured to provide limited liability to investors. The syndicator is the CTA or a CPO, and usually the general partner as well. These can be public or private. Private LPs are usually formed by a small group of wealthy investors, while public LPs attract large numbers of small ($2,000 to $5,000 minimum) investors. The latter requires a full-fledged prospectus and is more stringently watched by federal regulators. Both must be registered with the SEC.

The advantage to the investor is limited liability. The maximum loss is the amount invested. The negative side is liquidity. There is not always an active aftermarket for LP interests. Once in, you may have problems getting out. Also, the gains and losses are considered passive and can be used only to offset other passive losses or gains. The general partner, which may be a corporation, assumes the overall risk, but these programs often include a 50 percent deadman switch. If the losses reach or exceed 50 percent of the equity, trading ceases. This is a common feature in just about all programs to protect the CTA as well as the investors.

The private LP is an excellent vehicle for a close-knit group of 10 or so wealthy investors. Each, for example, contributes a half million dollars. With a total pool of $5 million, it is economical to hire a trading manager to select and monitor several CTAs. The size helps manage the systematic risk of the futures market.

Regulation D Offering

There are certain classes of securities that are exempt from the Securities Act of 1933. One of these, commonly used as an investment medium to trade futures, is known as Reg D Offerings. Regulation D of the 1933 Act covers private placements. Under Reg D is Rule 506, which exempts issues from SEC registration if they are sold to no more than 35 nonaccredited or unqualified investors.

A qualified investor has a net worth of $1 million or more, has made at least $200,000 or more in each of the two preceding years (or $300,000 if jointly with spouse), and has a reasonable expectation of making that much again in the year of investment. In other words, only the wealthy need apply. The reason is the lawmakers felt that if you amassed $1 million in net worth, you could protect yourself. It's interesting to note that the $1 million figure has not been adjusted for inflation since 1933. What a difference six decades has made to the buying power of a million bucks!

There was no exemption given to the type of information an investor must receive nor to the tax, fraud, and misrepresentation portion of the Act. A private placement memo replaces the traditional prospectus. The reason why this type of offering is popular is the reduced cost of a full-fledged SEC registration and that there is no limitation on the amount that can be raised. The downside to the investor is illiquidity, but liability is limited to the amount invested.

A first cousin of Reg D is the Rule 147 offering. These are sold entirely in one state and are exempt from SEC registration under Rule 147. The state commissioner of securities has jurisdiction. Once again, liquidity can be a problem for investors. As with the Reg D, a private placement memorandum details the offering.

Regulatory Recourse

Knowing the type of investment you enter tells you who governs the regulatory process. For example, the simple managed futures trading program would be between yourself, a broker, and someone doing the trading, which could also be the broker. No security is issued. Therefore, the primarily regulators would be the NFA and the CFTC.

As we progress, the offerings become a security, perhaps exempt from SEC registration, but a security nonetheless. In these cases, the SEC, the NASD, and the state commissioner of securities are the primary regulators during the selling period. Once trading begins, it is under the jurisdiction of the NFA and CFTC. This is the general rule and is not a legal opinion of any sort.

As an investor, you have recourse to all of the following, depending on the type of investment you make:

- Securities and Exchange Commission (SEC)
- Commodity Futures Trading Commission (CFTC)
- National Association of Securities Dealers (NASD)
- National Future Association (NFA)
- State Security Commission
- State Courts
- Federal Courts

The route you take depends on how serious your complaint is and the advice you get from your attorney.

For simple disputes about trades or commissions, the futures industry regulators have well-established procedures. For example, if you had a unresolved problem in your futures account, you could call the NFA's toll-free number for advice and information about specific regulation covering the situation. They'd offer to put you in touch with a trained mediator and send you a copy of their booklet *A Guide to Arbitration of Customer Disputes.* The mediator listens to your side of the story and contacts the brokers, CTA, or brokerage firm(s) involved for their input. An attempt would be made to resolve the issue to everyone's satisfaction.

If the results of mediation are unsatisfactory, you can compel the broker and his or her firm to binding arbitration with the NFA. This would be before a panel and you could specify that some members be public, i.e., not affiliated with the futures industry. The objective of arbitration is to obtain swift, fair, and inexpensive resolution of a simple dispute. It is considered inexpensive because a lawyer is not required and the rules of evidence are not strict, as they would be at a trial. Additionally, arbitration can take place by phone, so travel costs are avoided. This can be important if you are not near a major financial center.

A second avenue of recourse with futures disputes is the CFTC. They also have a booklet on the subject, entitled *Questions and Answers about How You Can Resolve a Commodity Market-Related Dispute.* It explains the CFTC's three reparation procedures.

- Voluntary
- Summary
- Formal

The voluntary procedure is used for claims under $10,000. It is administered by judgment officers appointed by the CFTC. Both parties have an opportunity to uncover facts ("discovery") and present their arguments in writing. There is no oral hearing. Decisions are final, and no appeal is permitted. A nonrefundable $25 fee is required.

The summary procedure is similar to the voluntary, but it allows for both a limited oral presentation and a written presentation, which takes place in Washington, DC. Further, you can appeal the decision to the CFTC and to a court of law if you are still not satisfied. It handles complaints of $10,000 or less and requires a $50 nonrefundable filing fee.

The formal procedure is designed to handle major complaints— over $10,000. A courtlike hearing is conducted in one of 20 locations throughout the United States before an administrative judge. You can be represented by an attorney if you wish. Appeals to the CFTC and the courts are possible. A $200 nonrefundable fee is required to file.

Besides the NFA and the CFTC, you can take a complaint to the American Arbitration Association or file a civil suit. If you think your broker or his or her firm has committed a criminal offense, you can contact the Federal Bureau of Investigation (FBI) or, if the U.S. mail was involved, the Chief Postal Inspector of the United States Postal Service.

If you are invested in a limited partnership or a fund, you may be able to appeal to your local state attorney general or the Securities and Exchange Commission. Other places with which you may check are the Better Business Bureau and the Federal Trade Commission.

For help deciding your most effective alternative, you need to sit down and discuss it with your attorney. In our opinion, your most effective protection results from systematically conducting due diligence research when selecting a CTA, a trading program (LP, etc.), and a broker. Act with reason—don't get caught up in an emotional response to the CTA's track record.

The most beneficial negotiations are done, in our opinion, between customer and client. Once it goes beyond this stage, the costs and complications often outweigh the results. Our advice is to work hard at this level to keep the lines of communication open.

You may be wondering what can be considered as grounds for a legitimate complaint. Losing money? Bad advice? A trade gone sour? An honest error? None of the above. All these should be expected. Anyone who has ever traded will attest that losing money on some trades is part of the nature of the beast. Bad advice simply means your CTA, or his or her company's research, cannot foretell the future accurately. Nobody can. This shouldn't be a surprise either. The following are some of the grounds for a formal complaint:

- Being high-pressured into opening an account
- Receiving unreasonable promises, such as "This CTA is guaranteed to make you big bucks!"
- Any fraudulent or deceitful communications made to you by your CTA or his or her firm
- Excessive trading in your account
- Uncorrected errors in your account

If you have an account that a third party is trading, you can ask the FCM, via the broker, to send you duplicate statements. With pools, LPs, and funds, this is not possible. You have a syndicator that is responsible for checking everything. By monitoring the duplicate statements, you can catch most errors. You want to check to see:

- Are the commissions charged correct?
- Is the strategy agreed upon with the CTA or trader being followed?

- Are any markets you told the CTA to avoid being traded?

It doesn't hurt once in a while to go over daily or monthly statements with your trader. Let him or her know you're monitoring the trading closely. Most importantly, you have every right to do this because it's your money at risk.

15

Putting It All Together—
Four Scenarios

To provide an insight into how professional trading managers structure and manage futures trading programs for their clients, we are going to describe the investment needs of four distinctly different investor types and discuss how each situation could be approached, plus any special circumstances that should be addressed.

We are doing this for illustrative and educational purposes only. This is not an offer to sell any program mentioned. Sales of professionally managed programs are done via disclosure document, prospectus, or offering memorandum. Never invest without reading all the documentation carefully. By the time you read this book, all the data will be outdated. Some of the trading systems may no longer be available and those that are structured as securities (limited partnerships, Reg D offerings, etc.) may not be registered in the state in which you live. Therefore, you could not invest in them even if you wanted to. All we are attempting to do is illustrate the thought process involved.

Scenario One—The Individual Investor

This individual has talked to several commodity brokers and security firms in the last six months. He has chosen "our" firm to assist him in placing some funds in a managed futures program. Let's assume we just completed an in-depth interview. This person has done a good job of building a firm financial foundation. All of the components of a balanced portfolio are in place—home, insurance, retirement plan, and investments. The investment portfolio is currently valued at $500,000 and is allocated as follows:

Current Investment Portfolio

Stocks	$200,000.00
Bonds	$100,000.00
Real Estate, LPs, etc.	$100,000.00
Collectibles	$25,000.00
Cash	$75,000.00

The annual return to the portfolio has been in the 12 percent–15 percent range. This investor has decided to invest 10 percent of the portfolio, or $50,000 of the cash portion, in managed futures with the following objectives:

- Preservation of capital is a primary consideration.
- The ideal annual rate of return should be twice the current rate the portfolio is earning.
- The program should also provide some protection against adverse movements of the stock and bond portions of the portfolio.
- Some exposure to foreign and physical commodities would add additional balance to the overall portfolio.

We make several passes through our asset-allocation software and generate an efficient frontier on the current asset allocation (see Exhibit 15.1) for a baseline. The computer also flags several possible futures programs that fit our client's needs, one of which is the SCI

EXHIBIT 15.1

Efficient Frontier

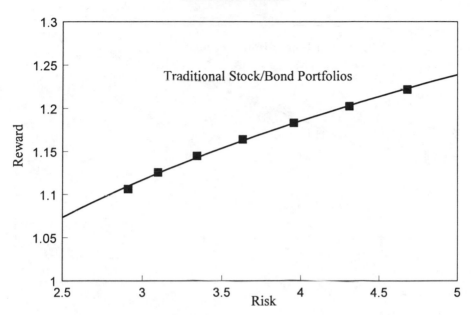

Source: SCI Capital Management, Cedar Rapids, IA.

Leveraged Allocation Fund I, L.P. (SCI Fund). At this point, we do another efficient frontier analysis to determine the impact of adding the SCI Fund to the portfolio (see Exhibit 15.2). Since there is an improvement, we proceed.

The first and foremost objective is the preservation of capital. Since the program selected is a limited partnership, the maximum loss our investor could sustain is 100 percent of the amount invested. Loss cannot exceed the amount pledged or guaranteed by the limited partnership. Additionally, the SCI Fund has a proviso to suspend trading if the net asset value (NAV) drops below 50 percent of its *highest* NAV. If this investor put $50,000 into this fund, the maximum

EXHIBIT 15.2

Efficient Frontier

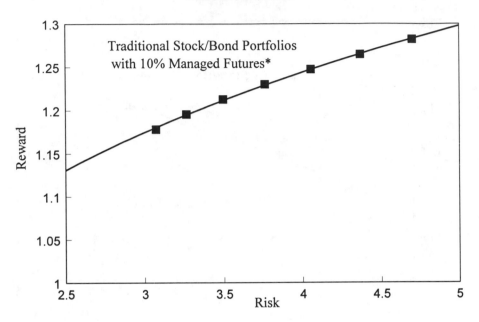

Traditional Stock/Bond Portfolios with 10% Managed Futures*

* SCI Capital Management's Associates Leveraged Growth Fund

Source: SCI Capital Management, Cedar Rapids, IA.

loss, if the "deadman switch" works properly, would be approximately $25,000, or 5 percent of the investment portfolio.

We also like the SCI Fund's approach to leveraging for this particular client. A four-to-one ratio is maintained. This means that the total market value of the futures contracts shall not exceed five times the equity in the account. And, as much equity as possible is held in U.S. Treasury bills to generate interest income.

The SCI Fund characterizes itself as a price trend anticipator. It attempts to project the futures price of the contracts it trades and establish long positions if the projection indicates higher prices ahead. The fund sells short when it forecasts a downtrend. Proprie-

EXHIBIT 15.3
S&P 500 Forecasting Model

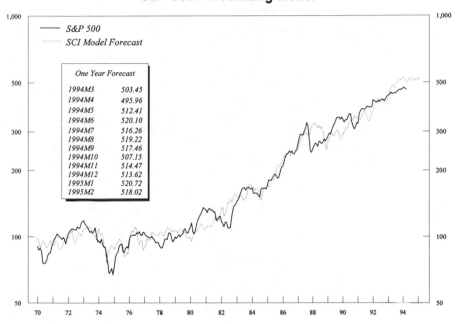

One Year Forecast	
1994M3	503.45
1994M4	495.96
1994M5	512.41
1994M6	520.10
1994M7	516.26
1994M8	519.22
1994M9	517.46
1994M10	507.15
1994M11	514.47
1994M12	513.62
1995M1	520.72
1995M2	518.02

Source: SCI Capital Management, Cedar Rapids, IA.

tary forecasting models, for each of the four markets it trades, drive the system. These computer simulations attempt to forecast the trends of the Standard and Poor's 500, KR-CRB-Goldman Sachs Commodity (these are traded as if they were one index) Indexes, U.S. Treasury Bond Yield, and the U.S. Trade-Weighted Dollar Indexes. (See Exhibits 15.3, 15.4, 15.5, and 15.6.) The fund manager believes this combination provides a balanced portfolio. The following correlation coefficients bear this out:

January 1970 to December 1987

	Stocks	Bonds	Bills	Futures	Forex
Stocks	1.000	0.327	–0.100	0.006	–0.091
Bonds		1.000	–0.009	–0.167	–0.086

EXHIBIT 15.4
KR-CRB Futures Index Forecasting Model

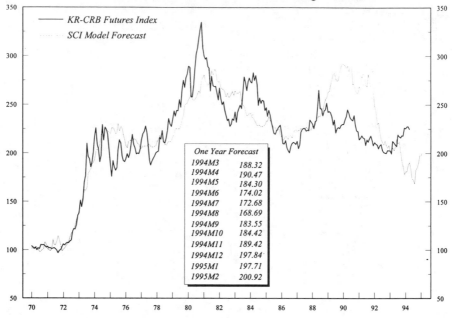

Source: SCI Capital Management, Cedar Rapids, IA.

	Stocks	Bonds	Bills	Futures	Forex
Bills			1.000	–0.149	–0.334
Futures				1.000	–0.059
Foreign Exchange (Forex)					1.000

Note stocks and bonds move together, confirming the data discussed earlier, while commodity futures are independent of stocks and negatively correlated to bonds. Foreign exchange rates, represented in the SCI Fund by the Dollar Index, are also uninfluenced by the stock or bond markets.

This investor gets exposure to all the major markets of the world through the structure of this fund. World currencies are reflected in

EXHIBIT 15.5
U.S. Treasury Bond Forecasting Model

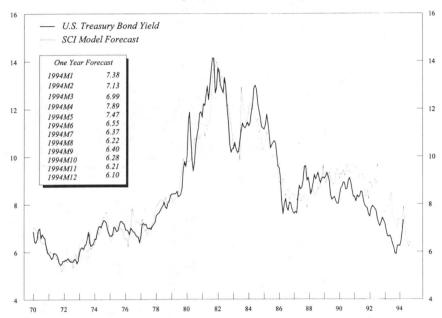

One Year Forecast	
1994M1	7.38
1994M2	7.13
1994M3	6.99
1994M4	7.89
1994M5	7.47
1994M6	6.55
1994M7	6.37
1994M8	6.22
1994M9	6.40
1994M10	6.28
1994M11	6.21
1994M12	6.10

Source: SCI Capital Management, Cedar Rapids, IA.

the dollar; physical commodities in the KR-CRB and Goldman Sachs Indexes; the stock market by the S&P 500; and the bond market via the U.S. long bond contract. We particularly like the structure of the physical commodity markets because the KR-CRB is heavily weighted toward the grains and the Goldman Sachs to the energies. The former reacts to weather-related emergencies, while the latter is politically sensitive. The investor also gets some downside hedging protection for the stock portion of his or her portfolio, since the fund would short the S&P 500 during major bear markets.

We classify the trading system the fund utilizes as systematic, which means the computerized signals are religiously followed, rather than a discretionary approach, which allows the chief trader to override signals. This approach accounts for the fund's discipline.

EXHIBIT 15.6
U.S. Dollar Forecasting Model

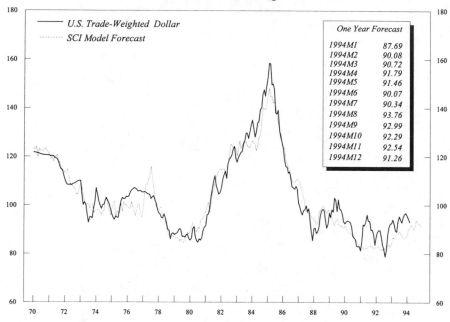

One Year Forecast	
1994M1	87.69
1994M2	90.08
1994M3	90.72
1994M4	91.79
1994M5	91.46
1994M6	90.07
1994M7	90.34
1994M8	93.76
1994M9	92.99
1994M10	92.29
1994M11	92.54
1994M12	91.26

Source: SCI Capital Management, Cedar Rapids, IA.

Part of this systematic approach is the allocation of equity among the four major trading segments. The computer divides the trading equity, from a minimum of 10 percent to a maximum of 45 percent, among the four markets. A typical allocation would look like this:

Short KR-CRB—GSCI Indexes	36%
Long S&P 500 Futures	29%
Short Trade-Weighted Dollar	21%
Long U.S. T-bond Futures	14%
Total	100%

We also like the fee structure of the fund, since it keeps the per trade brokerage charge down to only $10 per round turn. Other fees include 5 percent on the front end, 2 percent annual management, 3 percent service, and 10 percent trading incentive on new trading profits. The annual return, since inception in February of 1986, falls within the range our investor specified, averaging 1.87 percent per month, or just over 22 percent a year.

All in all, the SCI Fund appears to satisfy the needs expressed by the client. Again, it was one of several that matched the criteria. The investor would be presented with all the possibilities and he or she would make the final decision.

Scenario Two—The Large Investor

A large investor has $700,000 (10 percent of her total investment portfolio) to invest in managed futures programs. Besides wanting to give her current portfolio's ROR some vitality, preservation of capital is uppermost in her thoughts. This individual is adventuresome, but not foolhardy.

For this investor, we'd recommend selecting seven separate managed futures programs of approximately $100,000 each. Our rationale is as follows: Let's say one CTA blows out in any given year, losing 50 percent of the $100,000 entrusted to him or her. The other six CTAs would need to average 8.3 percent for that year to earn back the $50,000 lost. Or if two CTAs self-destructed in the same year, the other five would have to generate 20 percent that year to recoup the $100,000 given up to the market by the other two.

We would be very comfortable with these odds for several reasons. First, the CTAs would be carefully chosen, using the following criteria:

- Successful track records over at least the last three years, or preferably five years, with average annual RORs of approximately 25 percent or more
- Largest historical drawdown less than 50 percent
- Satisfactory ratios, particularly the winning months to losing and gains to losses

- Volatility rating no higher than the medium range
- Strong back office

Most importantly, the seven CTAs would be either neutral or negatively correlated to each other. For example, some would be discretionary traders, others systematic. Trend followers would be balanced by trend anticipators; technical analysts with fundamentalists. Even the market specialties would be noncorrelated—grains vs. meats vs. metals vs. softs vs. energies vs. currencies vs. financials vs. indexes, etc. Nothing would be left to chance.

Our objective is to manage both the systematic and unsystematic risk of the futures markets. The key to a successful portfolio is selecting a diversified team of professional, experienced CTAs with strong and long track records for rates of return and volatility.

Scenario Three—The Syndication

A group of 10 investors decide to form a limited partnership to trade futures, but none of them has the time or experience to act as general partner (GP). Nor does anyone want to assume the unlimited risk that falls on the shoulders of the GP. They take this challenge to a commodity pool operator (CPO).

A CPO is an individual, corporation, or organization in the business of operating and promoting commodity pools. On occasion, a CTA can also be a CPO who promotes his or her own trading programs. In this case, our investors seek a CPO independent of CTAs. They take this approach to get an unbiased analysis of potential traders.

CPOs are required to register with the NFA, unless the total capital contribution to all pools they manage is less than $200,000 *and* there are no more than 15 participants in any one pool. Earlier we discussed the advantages of dealing with registered entities, such as customer complaint resolution procedures. All these hold true here, and there are several more.

Probably the most important is the financial control the NFA has over its registrants, backed by its ability to conduct unannounced audits. CPOs are required to establish and maintain routine accounting records (cash receipt, dispersement, and general journals and ledgers), plus a special ledger on each pool they control. This daily ledger contains an itemized record of each transaction, including date, quantity, commodity, price, the FCM carrying the account, the IB (if applicable), whether the commodity interest was purchased or sold, and the gain/loss realized. For options, the record indicates if it was a put/call, strike price, or premium, and the expiration date. All records received from FCMs and CTAs must be kept. Records of the CPO's, and its principals', personal trading accounts are open to inspection by the NFA. On demand, the CPO must produce canceled checks, bank statements, invoices, computer-generated records, statements, and almost any pool-related documents the NFA requests, such as copies of sales promotional materials, advertisements, and correspondence. If there is a problem, the NFA has the authority to resolve it and this is why these investors went the CPO route.

They were also interested in the reporting and tracking capabilities of CPOs, since none of them have the time or experience to do it properly. For example, CPOs must distribute account statements within thirty days of the end of the accounting period, in this case monthly. Annual reports are also mandatory and are due by 45 days after the end of the fiscal year, which could be set to meet the tax needs of the investors. The annual report must include statements of income or loss and changes in net asset value.

They also found it comforting to learn that CPOs must reveal any material dealings between themselves and the pool, the CTAs selected to do the actual trading, and all other individuals or organizations involved, such as FCMs, IBs, brokers, etc. It is always good to know who is getting any part of the action. This way, unneeded expenses can be kept to a minimum. Even the annual report must be certified by an independent public accountant.

As for tracking, most CPOs keep in daily contact with the CTAs doing the actual trading. They review daily computer runs of all transactions. Some use sophisticated computer models to make sure pools are balanced as to traders and markets. As we learned, diversification as to CTA trading styles (systematic vs. discretionary) as well as to markets traded (financials vs. grains vs. energies, etc.) is important. The best CPOs know their CTAs up close and personal. They know who's sick, tired, having personal problems—there isn't anything that doesn't impact trading. Most importantly, they know when to change CTAs and when to weather out storms.

All this analysis, paperwork, reporting, oversight—not to mention the equipment and staff—costs money. CPOs usually charge a monthly management fee as a percentage of funds in the pools. In most cases, it is well worth it, particularly if you do not have the capabilities and experience to do it yourself. Fees are generally in line with those charged by financial managers on the security side of the business.

Last of all is the formation of the limited partnership itself. Some CPOs are attorneys and can do this themselves. Others farm it out, or the investment group provides their own attorney. One of the key issues to pay particular attention to is the transfer or partnership interests to new partners, if they are needed.

Scenario Four—The Qualified Pension Plan

For the fourth scenario, we chose a qualified pension plan for the following reasons:

1. A lot of very well-known companies are adding managed futures to their investment portfolios for the reasons already documented in this book, particularly because they can often increase the overall return while reducing risk. For example, some of the corporations currently using managed futures are Intel, Libby Owens Ford, Weyerhauser, World Bank, and Virginia Supplemental Retirement System.

2. These plans are highly regulated by the Department of Labor, IRS, SEC, CFTC, and state banking, insurance, and securities agencies. All these organizations scrutinize the investment practices of these plans for the protection of the employees who invest. If managed futures can pass the muster of all this regulatory oversight, there must be something worth consideration for just about every serious investor.

We were careful to use the term "qualified" pension plan. "Qualified" means contributions of employees and employers are tax deductible under IRS rules. Since they are tax deductible, the federal government has a right of oversight.

Besides the tax code, the federal government's authority emanates from the Employee Retirement Income Security Act of 1974 (ERISA). ERISA was enacted to protect corporate and union retirement plan participants against mismanagement of retirement funds and to ensure equitable participation of all employees from the top brass to the custodians. The administration of ERISA is the province of the Department of Labor.

As far as managing money is concerned, one of the key issues with ERISA and other related labor law is the "Prudent Man Rule." Fiduciaries of plans must act with care, skill, prudence, and diligence when selecting investments (and all other duties) for the funds, as a prudent man would when acting in a similar capacity and familiar with such matters in similar circumstances.

The obvious question is whether investing in futures is prudent or not. The Labor Department has decided against publishing a list of "safe harbor" investments allowable in pensions plans, as are available in some other financial areas. Its approach has been that the ERISA fiduciary's investment decisions should be evaluated as to their impact on the whole of the fund—not individually.

This position is very critical in the selection of CTAs to manage a portion of a fund, and even more important in the selection of the trading advisor to manage the CTAs. Is it prudent or imprudent to sell the T-bond short? At first glance, one would have to say shorting a very volatile market such as this one would be extremely imprudent. But what if the fund in question owned hundreds of millions of dollars' worth of bonds? All of a sudden, shorting bonds or buying some put options to hedge the risk of interest rates going higher, driving the value of the bonds lower, sounds prudent—almost downright smart!

This same argument holds true when the entire portfolio of the fund is analyzed to determine its efficient frontier. What profitable investments are available to the fund that are negatively correlated to its traditional stock/bond portfolio? One of the answers, as we have already learned, is managed futures. Used properly, they can be a prudent investment for a pension plan, in our opinion.

There are a few other sticky wickets, or Macro-Disqualifiers, fund administrators must negotiate. For example, a fiduciary must act *solely* in the interest of participants and beneficiaries and keep expenses to the minimum. Additionally, the fiduciary is prohibited from self-dealing, acting as a party with a competing or adverse interest in the plan, and receiving any compensation from any other party other than the plan. In other words, neither the FCM nor the trading manager should be named as a fiduciary. Both of these entities are expected to cross-trade (represent both sides of a futures trade by brokering for customers who are long and others short), work on an incentive fee basis (a conflict of interest with the pension fund), and provide a variety of services with compensation from multiple sources—all in the normal course of one business day.

Fiduciaries have two additional duties that impact managed futures: diversification and documentation. It is their responsibility to see that the fund they supervise is balanced so as to minimize the risks of loss, unless they can show it is clearly prudent not to do so. On this count, it has been demonstrated that managed futures, because of its negative correlation to traditional investments, enhances diversification.

Documentation has two meanings for fiduciaries. First, they must follow as exactly as possible the plan for the fund as it is spelled out in the fund's documentation. Secondly, they must always be prepared to substantiate their actions.

In the first situation, the plan for the pension may need to be amended before permitting an investment in managed futures. Depending on the individuals involved and the structure of the plan, this could be a simple or an impossible task. In some cases, it is impossible and becomes a Macro-Disqualifier. At other times, all it takes is a five-minute meeting of the trustees.

The second part of the documentation can be easily dealt with, but should not be taken lightly. The usual procedure, if capabilities are not present in-house, is to hire a consulting firm specializing in asset allocation. Remember the first two commandments of ERISA—be prudent and be able to prove it. The consultant needs to have access to a complete database of CTAs. The current asset allocation of the fund is inputted into the asset allocation model and an optimum efficient frontier is created. This allocation is then modified with the addition of various CTA teams, who have to be selected on the basis of the quality of their trading and their negative correlation to one another.

One of the most common questions asked by pension fund managers involves how a pension plan, whose assets are required by law to be held in trust, can have funds with an FCM that is not a fiduciary. Additionally, the FCM, by CFTC regulation, must be able to commit those funds to the market at a moment's notice to meet a margin call. All this sounds like a major conflict between ERISA and the CFTC. The Department of Labor solved this problem in 1982. It held that assets used by an FCM for margin were not plan assets for the purposes of the fiduciary requirements of ERISA. Nevertheless, fiduciaries must promptly sweep all excess margin from futures trading accounts.

The last question we need to touch on is whether the fiduciaries of ERISA pooled investment vehicles, such as master funds, common trust funds, mutual funds, etc., are required to comply with CFTC rules governing commodity pool operators (CPOs). An exclusion is available if these pools are not available to the public, use futures and options solely as a hedge, submit to special calls made by the CFTC, and certain percentages of total asset limitations are maintained.

Checklist for Pension Funds Investing in Managed Futures

This is a brief guide to the major issues that must be addressed before a pension fund invests in a managed futures program:

- *Risk vs. Reward Analysis*—Step one is to do some serious analysis to determine the increase in return and the reduction in volatility that can be expected from the addition of managed futures to the current asset allocation mix.

- *Legalities*—A wide array of state (insurance, security, labor, security) and federal (Dept. of Labor, SEC, CFTC, IRS) agencies are involved. The first step is to prepare an assessment of which agencies are involved and to what extent. An estimate of the cost and problems of compliance with each jurisdiction needs to be presented to the trustees.

- *Documentation*—The plan and trust agreement must be reviewed to see what changes, if any, would be required. Proper authorization from the board of directors or trustees would be required.

- *Preliminary Trading Plan*—This would detail the trading objectives and limitations to be placed on the commodity trading advisors, as well as a policy statement.

- *Management and Control*—Specific procedures should be prepared for the records that will be kept, adjustments to accounting, the tracking system, and any special personnel, equipment, or reports required.

- *Evaluation*—The criteria to measure the success or failure of the project should be clearly set out in writing in advance.

Conclusion

We've spent a lot of time talking about loss, risk, and volatility. These are important considerations because futures trading is a very speculative investment. By now you may be wondering why there is so much excitement about managed futures. Why are some of the leading CTAs refusing to take additional funds from investors and why are some CTAs only distributing profits? The last three illustrations may explain what many of the world's most savvy investors have learned about investing in derivatives.

Exhibit 15.7 quantifies the risk, using standard deviation as the measurement, and compares managed futures to the U.S. stock market, the bond market, and an index of foreign stocks. The Barclay CTA Index, which represents a large portfolio of CTAs, has the high-

EXHIBIT 15.7
Standard Deviation of Monthly Returns
1980–1993

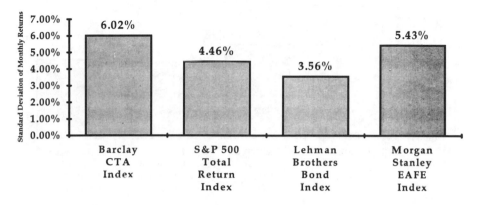

Source: Barclay Trading Group, Ltd., Fairfield, IA.

est SD. But if you look at Exhibits 15.8 and 15.9, you'll also see that managed futures has the highest return and the lowest peak to valley drawdown. Couple these facts with its negative or neutral correlation to the world's stock/bond markets and you begin to understand why investments among individuals and institutions in managed futures are growing so fast.

EXHIBIT 15.8
Compound Annual Returns
1980–1993

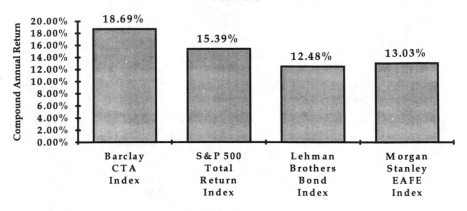

Source: Barclay Trading Group, Ltd., Fairfield, IA.

EXHIBIT 15.9
Worst Peak to Valley Loss
1980–1993

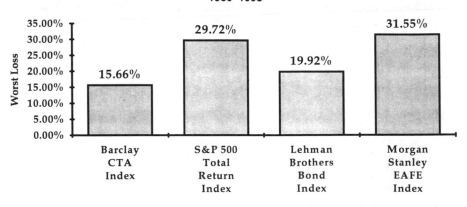

Source: Barclay Trading Group, Ltd., Fairfield, IA.

A Brief Chronology of the Managed Futures Industry

The following is a summary of a booklet produced by the Managed Futures Association, entitled *Major Events in the History of the Managed Futures Industry*, by Thomas Northcote. Mr. Northcote received special assistance in compiling this history from the following: Frank Pusateri, Jon Krass, Keith Campbell, Dennis Dunn, Darrell Jobman, Kate Rice, and the futures exchanges. Our thanks to the Association for supplying us with a copy of the booklet and all the other information it provided.

1930—Richard Donchian, the undisputed father of the Managed Futures Industry, began his Wall Street career. He was the developer of the first commodity system and the first commodity fund.

1937—Commodity Research Bureau (CRB) is founded by William Jiler and his two brothers. It's commodity price charting service, now owned by Knight-Ridder, is still widely used within the industry. CRB also published one of the first advisory newsletters and developed one of the earliest computerized databases. It has published a *Commodity Year Book*, filled with all the key statistics by commodity, since 1940. CTAs are indebted to CRB for generating and disseminating the analytical tools and data needed to drive trading systems.

1949—Futures, Inc., the first commodity fund, was formed by Richard Donchian. It traded at Hayden Stone until dissolved in 1975.

1952—In March, Harry J. Markowitz published an article entitled "Portfolio Selection" in *The Journal of Finance*. This was the beginning of the concept of Modern Portfolio Theory, which eventually embraced managed futures as an asset class to give certain investment portfolios balance. Mr. Markowitz received the Nobel Prize for Economics in 1990.

1953—Commodity News Service began providing news and price quotes, which is the life's blood of the commodity trader, to subscribers.

1955—The Futures Industry Association is formed. Its original name was the Association of Commodity Exchange Firms. The industry was large enough to support its own trade association.

1966—Dunn and Hargitt offer the first futures price database to the public.

1969—Commodities Corporation is founded. It is an industry think tank and is credited with finding and developing many successful CTAs.

1970—First two Regulation A (abbreviated SEC registration) commodity offerings are introduced to the public.
First broker-introduced managed account opened.

1971—Beginning of the financial futures markets with the introduction of foreign currency contracts. This segment grows incredibly fast and becomes popular with professional investors.

1972—*Futures Magazine* begins publication, as *Commodities Magazine*, by Leon Rose and Todd Loffon. The industry is large enough to support a trade publication.

1973—Wildly trending markets bring the general public's attention to the futures industry.

1974—Congress enacts the Commodity Exchange Act, which authorizes the CFTC. Previously, commodity markets were regulated by USDA (United States Department of Agriculture).

1975—Interest rate contracts, which become the most successful futures contract in history, begin trading.

1978—First multi-advisor pool is launched—the Thompson McKinnon Futures Fund.

1979—Gold hits its all-time high at $850 per ounce.

1980—National Association of Futures Trading Advisors formed.

1982—First stock index, the Value Line, begins trading at the Kansas City Board of Trade.
    Options are allowed to trade for the first time since being banned in the 1930s.
    National Futures Association begins operations.

1983—John Litner of Harvard University presents his study, which demonstrates how the addition of managed futures to a conventional stock/bond portfolio increases return while lowering volatility, to the Financial Analysts Federation's Annual Conference.

1985—The Commodity Exchange, Inc. (COMEX, New York) and the Sidney Futures Exchange establish a mutual offsetting link for their gold contracts. As this concept expands, it allows CTAs to trade more hours per day, giving them the option of entering or exiting positions during different trading sessions throughout the day or night. This can be important when market-moving events occur after normal trading hours for the CTA.

1986—First guaranteed public fund is offered—the Futures 1000 Fund.

The Managed Futures Trade Association is formed.

First pension fund, Detroit Policemen and Firemen's Pension Fund, invests in managed futures.

1988—CFTC permits CTAs to trade on foreign markets for the first time.

1989—Major banks enter managed futures arena—Chase Manhattan, Chemical, Continental, Citibank, Banque Indosuez, Society General, etc.

1990—Mint Investment Management is the first CTA to exceed $1 billion under management.

1991—National Association of Futures Trading Advisors and the Managed Futures Association merge into the Managed Futures Association with over 300 members.

Goldman Sachs Commodity Index is introduced.

Virginia Supplemental Retirement System allocates $100 million to managed futures.

ALCOA invests a portion of their fund in managed futures.

1992—Pension fund activity strong, as 19 pension funds invest in managed futures, i.e., AMP, Intel, Libby Owens Ford, Weyerhauser, World Banks, and others.

CFTC liberalizes offshore trading regulations for CTAs, as the futures markets spread across the globe.

Globex, an after-hours electronic trading exchange, begins operation.

1993—Funds invested in managed futures top $25 billion.

B

Sources of Additional Information

We categorized the informational sources. Hopefully, this will make it easier for you to find the additional assistance you need.

General Background Material:

One key skill in CTA selection is getting "inside the head" of prospective candidates. To do this you need to know what questions to ask and what is a meaningful answer. One of the best things to do before you visit, directly or via the telephone, with those on your short list is to read both of Jack Schwager's *Market Wizard* **books. Since they have been written in the interview format, they'll help you formulate questions and evaluate answers.**

Schwager, Jack D. *Market Wizards: Interviews with Top Traders.* (1989) New York Institute of Finance (Simon & Schuster), New York.

Schwager, Jack D. *The New Market Wizards: Conversations with America's Top Traders.* (1991) Harper Business (Harper Collins), New York.

If you need general information about the futures or stock markets, you might consider any of the following:

Bernstein, Jake. *Facts on Futures: Insights and Strategies for Winning in the Futures Markets.* (1987) Probus Publishing Company, Chicago.

Chance, Don M. *An Introduction to Options and Futures.* (1989) The Dryden Press, Chicago.

Gann, William D. *How to Make Profits in Commodities.* (1951) Lambert-Gann, Pomeroy, Washington.

Kaufman, Perry J. *Handbook of Futures Markets: Commodities, Financials, Stock Indexes, and Options.* (1984) John Wiley & Sons, Inc., New York.

Malkiel, Burton G. *A Random Walk down Wall Street.* (1990) W.W. Norton & Company, Inc., New York.

Markowitz, Harry. *Portfolio Selection: Efficient Diversification on Investments.* John Wiley & Sons, New York.

McCafferty, Thomas A., and Russell R. Wasendorf. *All About Futures from the Inside Out.* (1992) Probus Publishing Company, Chicago.

Natenberg, Sheldon. *Option Volatility & Pricing: Advanced Trading Strategies and Techniques.* Rev. ed. 1994. Probus Publishing Company, Chicago.

O'Higgins, Michael (with John Downes). *Beating the Dow.* (1991) Harper Collins Publishers, New York.

Schwager, Jack D. *A Complete Guide to the Futures Markets: Fundamental Analysis, Technical Analysis, Trading, Spreads, and Options.* (1984) John Wiley & Sons Inc., New York.

Siegel, Daniel R., and Diane F. Siegel. *The Futures Market.* (1990) Probus Publishing Company, Chicago.

For insights into the psychology of futures trading:

Bernstein, Jake. *The Investor's Quotient.* (1981) John Wiley & Sons, New York.

Mehrabian, Albert, Ph.D. *Your Inner Path to Investment Success: Insights in the Psychology of Investing.* (1991) Probus Publishing Company, Chicago.

Here are a few books specifically on managed futures:

Baratz, Morton. *The Investor's Guide to Futures Money Management.* (1989) LJR Communications, Inc., Columbia, Maryland.

Epstein, Charles B. (ed.) *Managed Futures in the Institutional Portfolio.* John Wiley & Sons, New York.

Managed Account Reports. *Reference Guide to Trading Advisors.* (1994) New York.

Peters, Carl C. (ed.) *Managed Futures—Performance, Evaluation, and Analysis of Commodity Funds, Pools, and Accounts.* (1992) Probus Publishing Company, Chicago.

Some newsletters and magazines to consider:

Barclay Institutional Report (Quarterly), Barclay Trading Group, Ltd. 508 Second Street, Suite 304, Fairfield, Iowa 52556 (515) 472-3456 or 1-800-338-2827.

Barclay Management Futures Report, Barclay Trading Group, Ltd. 508 Second Street, Suite 304, Fairfield, Iowa 52556 (515) 472-3456 or 1-800-338-2827.

BARRA/MLM Perspect, Mount Lucas Group, 47 Hulfish Street, P.O. Box 190, Princeton, New Jersey 08542 (609) 924-8868.

CMA Report, T. Young and Company, 326 White Oak Way, Santa Ynez, California 93460.

Commodity Traders Consumer Report, 1731 Howe Avenue, Sacramento, California 95825 (916) 677-7562.

Futures Magazine: Commodities, Options & Derivatives. Oster Communications, 219 Parkade, Cedar Falls, Iowa 50613.

F&OW (Futures & Options World for Global Financial & Commodity Derivatives Markets), c/o Royal Mail International, Yellowstone International, 87 Burlews Court, Hackensack, New Jersey 07601. Published at and by Metal Bulletin plc, Park Terrace, Worcester Park, UT47HY, United Kingdom. *F&OW* publish the *International Futures and Options Databook*.

Managed Account Reports, 220 Fifth Avenue, New York, New York 10001 (212) 213-6202 or 1-800-638-2525.

Managed Derivatives Magazine, Fourth Floor, Mitre House, 44-46 Fleet Street, London EC4Y IBN, United Kingdom.

Managed Futures International, c/o Peters Capital Management, 141 West Jackson Blvd., Suite 1679, Chicago, Illinois 60604 (312) 341-7051.

Managed Futures Today, P.O. Box 172, Glen Ridge, New Jersey 07028 (201) 744-0706.

Norwood Index Report, c/o Stark Research Inc., 1020 Prospect Street, Suite 3, La Jolla, California 92037 (619) 459-0818.

You may want to contact these databases for a copy of their sales literature to get an idea of what is available:

Barclay Trading Group, Ltd., 508 Second Street, Suite 304, Fairfield, Iowa 52556 (515) 472-3456 or 1-800-338-2827 ($5,000/year)

Christopher Resources, Inc., *The Complete Commodity Futures Directory*, 34 White Street, Box 488, Frankfort, Illinois 60423-0488 (708) 655-4923.

Irwin Tepper Associates, *Investment Policy Analyst*, 368 Highland Street, Newton, Massachusetts 02160 (617) 244-6747 ($5,000 for software).

LaPorte Asset Allocation, c/o Burlington Hall Asset Management, Inc., 126 Petersburg Road, Hackettstown, New Jersey 07840 (908) 852-1694 ($10,975/ year).

Prudential Securities CTA Reference, c/o SCI, 603 Commercial Street, Waterloo, Iowa 50701 (319) 234-6655 or 1-800-334-1206 (Information on CTAs available through futures brokers).

Sponsor Software System, *The Asset Allocation Expert*, 860 Fifth Avenue, New York, New York 10021 (212) 724-7535 ($4,500/year, no updating; $10,000 with quarterly updates).

Tass Management Ltd., 40 Catherine Place, London SWIE 6HL, United Kingdom (44) (71) 233-9797 ($12,000 to $18,500/year).

The following research papers may be of interest to you:

"Commodity Futures as a Hedge against Inflation," Z. Bodie, *The Journal of Portfolio Management*, Spring 1983, pp. 12-17.

"Futures and Options Trading for Pension Plans: The Regulatory Environment," Chicago Mercantile Exchange, 30 South Wacker, Chicago, Illinois 60606 (312) 930-1000.

"Justifying Managed Futures," Scott H. Irwin, *FIA Journal*, July/Aug. 1990, pp. 10–12.

"Managed Futures: An Institutional Investor's Primer," Gregory C. Allen, Callan Investments Institute, 71 Stevenson Street, Suite 1300, San Francisco, California 94105.

"Post-Modern Portfolio Theory Comes of Age," Brian M. Rom, *The Journal of Investing*, Institutional Investor, Inc., 488 Madison Avenue, New York, New York 10022.

"The Potential Role of Managed Commodity–Financial Futures Accounts (and/or Funds) in Portfolios of Stocks and Bonds," Presented by John Litner to the annual conference of the Financial Analysts Federation in Toronto, Canada on May 16, 1983.

"The Predictability of Managed Futures Returns," Scott H. Irwin, Barry A. Ward, and Carl R. Zulauf, presented at the Fourth Annual Managed Futures Symposium, Chicago, Illinois, 1992.

"Risk Premia and Price Volatility in Futures Markets," G. S. Maddala and Jisco Yoo, Center for the Study of Futures Markets, Columbia Business School, Columbia University, New York, New York.

All the futures exchanges have information available on managed futures. Additionally, their marketing departments will arrange tours of their facilities and introductions to CTAs:

AMEX Commodities Corporation, 86 Trinity Place, New York, New York 10006 (212) 306-8940.

Board of Trade of Kansas City, 4800 Main Street, Kansas City, Missouri 64112 (816) 753-7500.

Chicago Board of Trade, 141 West Jackson Blvd., Chicago, Illinois 60604 (312) 435-3620.

Chicago Mercantile Exchange, 30 South Wacker Drive, Chicago, Illinois 60606 (312) 930-1000.

Chicago Rice and Cotton Exchange, 444 West Jackson Blvd., Chicago, Illinois 60606 (312) 341-3078.

Coffee, Sugar & Cocoa Exchange, 4 World Trade Center, New York, New York 10048 (212) 938-2800.

Commodity Exchange Incorporated (COMEX), 4 World Trade Center, New York, New York 10048 (212) 938-2900.

MidAmerica Commodity Exchange, 141 West Jackson, Chicago, Illinois 60604 (312) 341-3000.

Minneapolis Grain Exchange, 150 Grain Exchange Building, Minneapolis, Minnesota 55415 (612) 338-6212.

New York Cotton Exchange, 4 World Trade Center, New York, New York 10048 (212) 938-2702.

New York Futures Exchange, 20 Broad Street, New York, New York 10005 (212) 656-4949.

New York Mercantile Exchange, 4 World Trade Center, New York, New York 10048 (212) 938-2222.

You may want to contact these organizations for information at some point:

Commodity Futures Trading Commission (CFTC), 2033 K Street NW, Washington, DC 20581 (202) 254-6387.

Futures Industry Association, 2001 Pennsylvania Ave., Washington, DC 20006 (202) 466-5460.

National Association of Securities Dealers (NASD), 1735 K Street NW, Washington, DC 20006 (202) 728-8044.

National Futures Association (NFA), 200 W. Madison Street, Suite 1600, Chicago, Illinois 60606 (312) 781-1410 or 1-800-621-3570.

Managed Futures Association, P.O. Box 287, Palo Alto, California 94302 (415) 325-4533.

Securities and Exchange Commission (SEC), 450 Fifth Street NW, Washington, DC 20006 (202) 728-8233.

Glossary of Terms

Actuals—The physical or cash commodity, as distinguished from commodity futures contracts.

Administrative law judge (ALJ)—A CFTC official authorized to conduct a proceeding and render a decision in a formal complaint procedure.

Aggregation—The policy under which all futures positions owned or controlled by one trader or a group of traders are combined to determine reporting status and speculative limit compliance.

Arbitrage—The simultaneous purchase of one commodity against the sale of another in order to profit from distortions from usual price relationships. *See also* Spread; Straddle.

Arbitration—A forum for the fair and impartial settlement of disputes that the parties involved are unable to resolve between themselves. NFA's arbitration program provides a forum for resolving futures-related disputes.

Associated person (AP)—An individual who solicits orders, customers, or customer funds on behalf of a Futures Commission Merchant, an Introducing Broker, a Commodity Trading Advisor, or a Commodity Pool Operator and who is registered with the Commodity Futures Trading Commission (CFTC) via the National Futures Association (NFA).

Asymmetrical risk evaluation—A method of measuring risk that skews the data being manipulated to the positive or negative, depending on which is predominant or more representative.

At the market. *See* Market order.

At-the-money—An option whose strike price is equal—or approximately equal—to the current market price of the underlying futures contract.

Averaging losers or down—The addition of new positions to currently losing ones to reduce the average cost of the overall position.

Award. *See* Reparations award.

Basis—The difference between the cash or spot price and the price of the nearby futures contract.

Bear market (bear/bearish)—A market in which prices are declining; a market participant who believes prices will move lower is called a "bear." A news item is considered bearish if it is expected to produce lower prices.

Bid—An offer to buy a specific quantity of a commodity at a stated price.

Board of trade—Any exchange or association of persons who are engaged in the business of buying or selling any commodity or receiving the same for sale on consignment. Usually means an exchange where commodity futures and/or options are traded. *See also* Contract market; Exchange.

Boiler room operation—An illegal or nearly illegal sales organization characterized by high-pressure telephone sales.

Break—A rapid and sharp price decline.

Broad tape—A term commonly applied to newswires carrying price and background information on securities and commodities markets, in contrast to exchanges' own price transmission wires, which use a narrow ticker tape.

Broker—A person paid a fee or commission for acting as an agent in making contracts or sales; a floor broker in commodities futures trading is a person who actually executes orders on the trading floor of an exchange; an account executive (associated person) is the person who deals with customers and their orders in commission house offices. *See* Registered commodity representative.

Brokerage—A fee charged by a broker for execution of a transaction; an amount per transaction or a percentage of the total value of the transaction; usually referred to as a commission fee.

Bucket, bucketing—Illegal practice of accepting orders to buy or sell without executing such orders; the illegal use of the customer's margin deposit without disclosing the fact of such use.

Bull market (bull/bullish)—A market in which prices are rising. A participant in futures who believes prices will move higher is called a "bull." A news item is considered bullish if it is expected to bring on higher prices.

Buy or sell on close or opening—To buy or sell at the end or the beginning of the trading session.

Buying hedge (or long hedge)—Buying futures contracts to protect against possible increased cost of commodities that will be needed in the future. *See* Hedging.

Call (option)—The buyer of a call option acquires the right but not the obligation to purchase a particular futures contract at a stated price on or before a particular date. Buyers of call options generally hope to profit from an increase in the futures price of the underlying commodity.

Car(s)—This is a colloquialism for futures contract(s). It came into common use when a railroad car or hopper of corn, wheat, etc., equaled the amount of a commodity in a futures contract. *See* Contract.

Carrying broker—A member of a commodity exchange, usually a clearinghouse member, through whom another broker or customer chooses to clear all or some trades.

Carrying charges—Costs incurred in warehousing the physical commodity, generally including interest, insurance, and storage.

Carryover—That part of the current supply of a commodity consisting of stocks from previous production/marketing seasons.

Cash commodity—Actual stocks of a commodity, as distinguished from futures contracts; goods available for immediate delivery or delivery within a specified period following sale; or a commodity bought or sold with an agreement for delivery at a specified future date. *See* Actuals; Forward contracting.

Cash forward sale. *See* Forward contracting.

Certificated stock—Stocks of a commodity that have been inspected and found to be of a quality deliverable against futures contracts, stored at the delivery points designated as regular or acceptable for delivery by the commodity exchange.

Charting—The use of graphs and charts in the technical analysis of futures markets to plot trends of price movements, average movements of price volume, and open interest. *See* Technical analysis.

Churning—Excessive trading of the customer's account by a broker who has control over the trading decisions for that account, to make more commissions while disregarding the best interests of the customer.

Clearing—The procedure through which trades are checked for accuracy after which the clearinghouse or association becomes the buyer to each seller of a futures contract, and the seller to each buyer.

Clearing member—A member of the clearinghouse or association. All trades of a nonclearing member must be registered and eventually settled through a clearing member.

Clearing Price. *See* Settlement price.

Clearinghouse—An agency connected with commodity exchanges through which all futures contracts are made, offset, or fulfilled through delivery of the actual commodity and through which financial settlement is made; often a fully chartered separate corporation, rather than a division of the exchange proper.

Close (the)—The period at the end of the trading session, officially designated by the exchange, during which all transactions are considered made "at the close."

Closing range—A range of closely related prices at which transactions took place at the closing of the market; buy and sell orders at the closing might have been filled at any point within such a range.

Commission—(1) A fee charged by a broker to a customer for performance of a specific duty, such as the buying or selling of futures contracts; (2) Sometimes used to refer to the Commodity Futures Trading Commission (CFTC).

Commission merchant—One who makes a trade, either for another member of the exchange or for a nonmember client, but who makes the trade in his or her own name and becomes liable as principal to the other party to the transaction.

Commodity—An entity of trade or commerce, services, or rights in which contracts for future delivery may be traded. Some of the contracts currently traded are wheat, corn, cotton, livestock, copper, gold, silver, oil, propane, plywood, currencies, Treasury bills, bonds, and notes.

Commodity Exchange Act—The federal act that provides for federal regulation of futures trading.

Commodity Futures Trading Commission (CFTC)—A commission set up by Congress to administer the Commodity Exchange Act, which regulates trading on commodity exchanges.

Commodity pool—An enterprise in which funds contributed by a number of persons are combined for the purpose of trading futures contracts and/or options on futures. Not the same as a joint account.

Commodity Pool Operator (CPO)—An individual or organization that operates or solicits funds for a commodity pool. Generally required to be registered with the Commodity Futures Trading Commission.

Commodity trading advisor (CTA)—An individual or firm that, for a fee, issues analysis or reports concerning commodities and advises others on the value or the advisability of trading in commodity futures, options, or leverage contracts.

Complainant—The individual who files a complaint seeking a reparations award against another individual or firm.

Confirmation statement—A statement sent by a commission house to a customer when a futures or options position has been initiated. The statement shows the number of contracts bought or sold and the prices at which the contracts were bought or sold. Sometimes combined with a purchase and sale statement.

Consolidation—A pause in trading activity in which price moves sideways, setting the stage for the next move. Traders evaluate their positions during periods of consolidation.

Contract—A term of reference describing a unit of trading for a commodity.

Contract grades—Standards or grades of commodities listed in the rules of the exchanges that must be met when delivering cash commodities against futures contracts. Grades are often accompanied by a schedule of discounts and premiums allowable for delivery of commodities of lesser or greater quality than the contract grade.

Contract market—A board of trade designated by the Commodity Futures Trading Commission to trade futures or option contracts on a particular commodity; commonly used to mean any exchange on which futures are traded. *See also* Board of trade; Exchange.

Contract month—The month in which delivery is to be made in accordance with a futures contract.

Controlled account. *See* Discretionary account.

Corner—To secure control of a commodity so that its price can be manipulated.

Correction—A price reaction against the prevailing trend of the market. Common corrections often amount to 33 percent, 50 percent, or 66 percent of the most recent trend movement; sometimes referred to as a retracement.

Correlation—The relationship between entities—such as CTAs, investments, indexes, etc. Entities are said to be correlated when they, their price, or their profitability move together or in sync.

Correlation coefficient—Usually a number ranging from +1 to –1 indicating the degree of simultaneous decrease or increase in the value of two entities. A CTA who trades grains based on weather would be negatively uncorrelated to a technical bond trader. The correlation coefficient would be at or near zero.

Cost of recovery—Administrative costs or expenses incurred in obtaining money due the complainant. Included are such costs as administrative fees, hearing room fees, charge for clerical services, travel expenses to attend the hearing, attorney's fees, filing costs, etc.

Covariance—Expected value of the deviations of corresponding values of two variables from their respective means, having the same sign as the correlation coefficient. Covariance numbers are unlimited in value.

Cover—To offset a previous futures transaction with an equal and opposite transaction. Short covering is a purchase of futures contracts to cover an earlier sale of an equal number of the same delivery month; liquidation is the sale of futures contracts to offset the obligation to take delivery on an equal number of futures contracts of the same delivery month purchased earlier.

Current delivery (month)—The futures contract that will come to maturity and become deliverable during the current month; also called "spot month."

Customer segregated funds. *See* Segregated account.

Day order—An order that if not executed expires automatically at the end of the trading session on the day it was entered.

Day traders—Commodity traders, generally members of the exchange active on the trading floor, who take positions in commodities and then liquidate them prior to the close of the trading day.

Dealer option—A put or call on a physical commodity, not originating on or subject to the rules of an exchange, written by a firm that deals in the underlying cash commodity.

Debit balance—Accounting condition where the trading losses in a customer's account exceed the amount of equity in the customer's account.

Deck—All of the unexecuted orders in a floor broker's possession.

Default—(1) In the futures market, the failure to perform on a futures contract as required by exchange rules, such as a failure to meet a margin call or to make or take delivery; (2) In reference to the federal farm loan program, the decision on the part of a producer of commodities not to repay the government loan, but instead to surrender his or her crops. This usually floods the market, driving prices lower.

Deferred delivery—The distant delivery months in which futures trading is taking place, as distinguished from the nearby futures delivery month.

Deliverable grades. *See* Contract grades.

Delivery—The tender and receipt of an actual commodity or warehouse receipt or other negotiable instrument covering such commodity, in settlement of a futures contract.

Delivery month—A calendar month during which a futures contract matures and becomes deliverable.

Delivery notice—Notice from the clearinghouse of a seller's intention to deliver the physical commodity against a short futures position; precedes and is distinct from the warehouse receipt or shipping certificate, which is the instrument of transfer of ownership.

Delivery points—Those locations designated by commodity exchanges at which stocks of a commodity represented by a futures contract may be delivered in fulfillment of the contract.

Delivery price—The official settlement price of the trading session during which the buyer of futures contracts receives through the clearinghouse a notice of the seller's intention to deliver, and the price at which the buyer must pay for the commodities represented by the futures contract.

Derivatives—Contracts and securities derived from conventional investments. Some examples are options on stocks or futures, swaps, forwards, mortgage-backed instruments. They are sometimes referred to as the "shadow markets" because they follow another market.

Discount—(1) A downward adjustment in price allowed for delivery of stocks of a commodity of lesser than deliverable grade against a futures contract; (2) sometimes used to refer to the price difference between futures of different delivery months, as in the phrase "July at a discount to May," indicating that the price of the July future is lower than that of the May.

Discovery—The process that allows one party to obtain information and documents relating to the dispute from the other party(ies) in the dispute.

Discretionary account—An arrangement by which the holder of the account gives written power of attorney to another, often a broker, to make buying and selling decisions without notification to the holder; often referred to as a managed account or controlled account.

Diversification—The spreading out of risk by trading several unrelated markets, investing in several asset classes or CTAs.

Drawdown—Loss of equity in an account.

Efficient frontier—The optimum mix of assets or traders to generate the highest return with the least amount of risk.

Elasticity—A characteristic of commodities that describes the interaction of the supply, demand, and price of a commodity. A commodity is said to be elastic in demand when a price change creates an increase or decrease in consumption. The supply of a commodity is said to be elastic when a change in price creates change in the production of the commodity. Inelasticity of supply or demand exists when either supply or demand is relatively unresponsive to changes in price.

Elliott Wave Theory—A technical analysis system devised by Ralph Nelson Elliott, which is based on markets moving in waves up and down. Each wave is subdivided into smaller waves. By knowing where your market is within the wave pattern, you can foretell the next price move.

Equity—The dollar value of a futures trading account if all open positions were offset at the going market price.

Exchange—An association of persons engaged in the business of buying and selling commodity futures and/or options. *See also* Board of trade; Contract market.

Exercise—Exercising an option means you elect to accept the underlying futures contract at the option's strike price.

Exercise price—The price at which the buyer of a call (put) option may choose to exercise his or her right to purchase (sell) the underlying futures contract; also called strike price.

Expiration date—Generally, the last date on which an option may be exercised.

FOB—Free on board; indicates that all delivery, inspection, and elevation or loading costs involved in putting commodities on board a carrier have been paid.

Feed ratios—The variable relationships of the cost of feeding animals to market weight sales prices, expressed in ratios, such as the hog/corn ratio. These serve as indicators of the profit return or lack of it in feeding animals to market weight.

Fibonacci number or sequence of numbers—The sequence of numbers (0,1,2,3,5,8,13,21,34,55,89,144,233 . . .) discovered by the Italian mathematician Leonardo de Pise in the thirteenth century, where the first two terms of the sequence are 0 and 1 and each successive number is the sum of the previous two numbers; the mathematical basis of the Elliott Wave Theory.

Fiduciary duty—Responsibility imposed by operation of law (from congressional policies underlying the Commodity Exchange Act) which requires that the broker act with special care in the handling of a customer's account.

First notice day—First day on which notices of intention to deliver cash commodities against futures contracts can be presented by sellers and received by buyers through the exchange clearinghouse.

Floor broker—An individual who executes orders on the trading floor of an exchange for any other person.

Floor traders—Members of an exchange who are personally present on the trading floors of exchanges to make trades for themselves and their customers; sometimes called scalpers or locals.

FOREX—This is the foreign exchange market that trades currencies.

Forwarding contracting—A cash transaction common in many industries, including commodities, in which the buyer and seller agree upon delivery of a specified quality and quantity of goods at a specified future date. Specific price may be agreed upon in advance or there may be agreements that the price will be determined at the time of delivery on the basis of either the prevailing local cash price or a futures price.

Free supply—Stocks of a commodity that are available from commercial sale, as distinguished from government-owned or controlled stocks.

Frontrunning—An unethical practice whereby a broker places his or her personal order in front of a customer's order that he thinks will move the market in his or her favor.

Fully disclosed—An account carried by the futures commission merchant in the name of the individual customer; opposite of an omnibus account.

Fundamental analysis—An approach to analysis of futures markets and commodity futures price trends that examines the underlying factors that will affect the supply and demand of the commodity being traded in futures. *See also* Technical analysis.

Futures commission merchant (FCM)—An individual or organization that solicits or accepts orders to buy or sell futures contracts or commodity options and accepts money or other assets from customers in connection with such orders. Must be registered with the Commodity Futures Trading Commission.

Futures contract—A standardized binding agreement to buy or sell a specified quantity or grade of a commodity at a later date, i.e., during a specified month. Futures contracts are freely transferable and can be traded only by public auction on designated exchanges.

Futures Industry Association (FIA)—The national trade association for the futures industry.

Gann analysis—A system of market forecasting based on the research of William Gann, who was well-known for his stock and commodity trading during the first half of the twentieth century.

Gap—A trading day during which the daily price range is completely above or below the previous day's range, causing a gap between them to be formed. Some traders then look for a retracement to "fill the gap."

Grantor—A person who sells an option and assumes the obligation but not the right, to sell (in the case of a call) or buy (in the case of a put) the underlying futures contract or commodity at the exercise price. *See also* Writer.

Gross processing margin (GPM)—Refers to the difference between the cost of soybeans and the combined sales income of the soybean oil and meal that results from processing soybeans.

Guided account—An account that is part of a program directed by a commodity trading advisor (CTA) or futures commission merchant (FCM). The CTA or FCM plans the trading strategies. The customer is advised to enter and/or liquidate specific trading positions. However, approval to enter the order must be given by the customer. These programs usually require a minimum initial investment and may include a trading strategy that will utilize only a part of the investment at any given time.

Hedge fund—Historically, it is a mutual fund that does some hedging. It has acquired a broader definition recently to include limited partnerships, as well as mutual funds, that sell short, arbitrage, and speculate.

Hedging—The sale of futures contracts in anticipation of future sales of cash commodities as a protection against possible price declines, or the purchase of futures contracts in anticipation of future purchases of cash commodities as a protection against increasing costs. *See also* Buying hedge; Selling hedge.

Illiquid—Thinly traded markets or investments, where there is a problem finding a buyer or seller.

Inelasticity—A characteristic that describes the interdependence of the supply, demand, and price of a commodity. A commodity is inelastic when a price change does not create an increase or decrease in consumption; inelasticity exists when supply and demand are relatively unresponsive to changes in price. *See also* Elasticity.

Implied volatility—The market's expectation of what volatility should be, based on current option prices.

Initial margin—A customer's funds required at the time a futures position is established, or an option is sold, to assure performance of the customer's obligations. Margin in commodities is not a down payment, as it is in securities. *See also* Margin.

Interbank—An informal, but highly structured, market used by major banks and a few very large CTAs for trading spot, options, and forwards in currencies and interest rate contracts.

In-the-money—An option having intrinsic value. A call is in-the-money if its strike price is below the current price of the underlying futures contract. A put is in-the-money if its strike price is above the current price of the underlying futures contract.

Intrinsic value—The absolute value of the in-the-money amount; that is, the amount that would be realized if an in-the-money option were exercised.

Introducing broker (IB)—A firm or individual that solicits and accepts commodity futures orders from customers but does not accept money, securities, or property from the customer. An IB must be registered with the Commodity Futures Trading Commission and must carry all of its accounts through an FCM on a fully disclosed basis.

Inverted market—Futures market in which the nearer months are selling at premiums over the more distant months; characteristically, a market in which supplies are currently in shortage.

Invisible supply—Uncounted stocks of a commodity in the hands of wholesalers, manufacturers, and producers that cannot be identified accurately; stocks outside commercial channels but theoretically available to the market.

Last trading day—Day on which trading ceases for the maturing (current) delivery month.

Leverage—The ability to control a large amount of an entity (stock, commodity, real estate, etc.) with a small goodwill deposit or down payment; essentially allows an investor to establish a position in the marketplace by depositing funds that are less than the value of the contract.

Leverage contract—A standardized agreement calling for the delivery of a commodity with payments against the total cost spread out over a period of time. Principal characteristics include: Standard units and quality of a commodity and of terms and conditions of the contract; payment and maintenance of margin; close out by offset or delivery (after payment in full); and no right to or interest in a specific lot of the commodity. Leverage contracts are not traded on exchanges.

Leverage transaction merchant (LTM)—The firm or individual through whom leverage contracts are entered. LTMs must be registered with the Commodity Futures Trading Commission.

Life of contract—Period between the beginning of trading in a particular future and the expiration of trading in the delivery month.

Limit. *See* Position limit; Price limit; Reporting limit; Variable limit.

Limit move—A price that has advanced or declined the limit permitted during one trading session as fixed by the rules of a contract market.

Limit order—An order in which the customer sets a limit on either price or time of execution, or both, as contrasted with a market order, which implies that the order should be filled at the most favorable price as soon as possible.

Liquidation—Usually the sale of futures contracts to offset the obligation to take delivery of an equal number of futures contracts of the same delivery month purchased earlier. Sometimes refers to the purchase of futures contracts to offset a previous sale.

Liquid market—A market where selling and buying can be accomplished easily due to the presence of many interested buyers and sellers.

Liquidity (or liquid market)—A broadly traded market where buying and selling can be accomplished with small price changes and bid and offer price spreads are narrow.

Loan program—Primary means of government agricultural price support operations, in which the government lends money to farmers at announced rates, with crops used as collateral. Default on these loans is the primary method by which the government acquires stocks of agricultural commodities.

Local—A name used for floor traders on the futures exchanges. An exchange member. Usually trades for own account. Function is to increase liquidity in markets.

Long—One who has bought a cash commodity or a commodity futures contract, in contrast to a short, who has sold a cash commodity or futures contract.

Long hedge—Buying futures contracts to protect against possible increased prices of commodities. *See also* Hedging.

Lot—A synonym for a futures contract. CTAs are said to trade "1 lot" or "50 lot," depending on their size.

Maintenance margin—The amount of money that must be maintained on deposit while a futures position is open. If the equity in a customer's account drops under the maintenance margin level, the broker must issue a call for money that will restore the customer's equity in the account to required initial levels. *See also* Margin.

Margin—In the futures industry, an amount of money deposited by both buyers and sellers of futures contracts to ensure performance against the contract. It is not a down payment.

Margin call—A call from a brokerage firm to a customer to bring margin deposits back up to minimum levels required by exchange regulations; similarly, a request by the clearinghouse to a clearing member firm to make additional deposits to bring clearing margins back to minimum levels required by clearinghouse rules.

Market order—An order to buy or sell futures contracts that is to be filled at the best possible price and as soon as possible, in contrast to a limit order, which may specify requirements for price or time of execution. *See also* Limit order.

Maturity—Period within which a futures contract can be settled by delivery of the actual commodity; the period between the first notice day and the last trading day of a commodity futures contract.

Maximum price fluctuation. *See* Limit move.

Mean variance—Usually the standard deviation around the mean or average.

Minimum price fluctuation. *See* Point.

Misrepresentation—An untrue or misleading statement concerning a material fact relied upon by a customer when making his/her decision about an investment.

Modern Portfolio Theory—The practice of allocating components within an investment portfolio among neutrally or negatively correlated assets to reduce risk and increase return. Harry Markowitz is the person given credit for developing and popularizing the theory.

Momentum indicator—A line that is plotted to represent the difference between today's price and the price of a fixed number of days ago. Momentum can be measured as the difference between today's price and the current value of a moving average. Often referred to as momentum oscillators.

Moving average—A mathematical procedure to smooth or eliminate the fluctuations in data. Moving averages emphasize the direction of a trend, confirm trend reversals, and smooth out price and volume fluctuations or "noise" that can confuse interpretation of the market.

National Association of Futures Trading Advisors (NAFTA)—The national trade association of Commodity Pool Operators (CPOs), Commodity Trading Advisors (CTAs), and related industry participants).

National Futures Association (NFA)—The industrywide self-regulatory organization of the futures industry.

Nearby delivery (month)—The futures contract closest to maturity.

Nearbys—The nearest delivery months of a futures market.

Net performance—An increase or decrease in net asset value exclusive of additions, withdrawals, and redemptions.

Net position—The difference between the open long (buy) contracts and the open short (sell) contracts held by any one person in any one futures contract month or in all months combined.

New asset value—The value of each unit of a commodity pool. Basically, a calculation of assets minus liabilities plus or minus the value of open positions (marked-to-the-market) divided by the number of units.

Nominal price—Declared price for a futures month, sometimes used in place of a closing price when no recent trading has taken place in that particular delivery month; usually an average of the bid and asked prices.

Nondisclosure—Failure to disclose a material fact needed by the customer to make a decision regarding an investment.

Normalizing—An adjustment to data, such as a price series, to put it within normal or more standard range. A technique used to develop a trading system.

Norwood Index—An index of the performance of public commodity funds created by Stark Research, Inc.

Notice day. *See* First notice day.

Notice of delivery. *See* Delivery notice.

Offer—An indication of willingness to sell at a given price; opposite of bid.

Offset—The liquidation of a purchase of futures through the sale of an equal number of contracts of the same delivery months, or the covering of a short sale of futures contracts through the purchase of an equal number of contracts of the same delivery month. Either action transfers the obligation to make or take delivery of the actual commodity to someone else.

Omnibus account—An account carried by one futures commission merchant with another in which the transactions of two or more persons are combined, rather than designated separately, and the identity of the individual accounts is not disclosed.

Open—The period at the beginning of the trading session officially designated by the exchange during which all transactions are considered made "at the open."

Open interest—The total number of futures contracts of a given commodity which have not yet been offset by opposite futures transactions nor fulfilled by delivery of the actual commodity; the total number of open transactions, with each transaction having a buyer and a seller.

Open outcry—Method of public auction for making bids and offers in the trading pits or rings of commodity exchanges.

Open trade equity—The unrealized gain or loss on open positions.

Opening range—Range of closely related prices at which transactions took place at the opening of the market; buying and selling orders at the opening might be filled at any point within such a range.

Optimizing portfolio efficiency—Determining the ideal mix of assets within a portfolio to generate the highest return with the least amount of risk.

Option contract—A unilateral contract that gives the buyer the right, but not the obligation, to buy or sell a specified quantity of a commodity or a futures contract at a specific price within a specified period of time, regardless of the market price of that commodity or futures contract. The seller of the option has the obligation to sell the commodity or futures contract or buy it from the option buyer at the exercise price if the option is exercised. *See also* Call (option); Put (option).

Option premium—The money, securities, or property the buyer pays to the writer (grantor) for granting an option contract.

Option seller. *See* Grantor.

Order execution—Handling of a customer order by a broker—includes receiving the order verbally or in writing from the customer, transmitting it to the trading floor of the exchange where the transaction takes place, and returning confirmation (fill price) of the completed order to the customer.

Orders. *See* Market order; Stop order.

Original margin—Term applied to the initial deposit of margin money required of clearing member firms by clearinghouse rules; parallels the initial margin deposit required of customers.

Out-of-the-money—A call option with a strike price higher or a put option with a strike price lower than the current market value of the underlying asset.

Overbought—A technical opinion that the market price has risen too steeply and too fast in relation to underlying fundamental factors.

Oversold—A technical opinion that the market price has declined too steeply and too fast in relation to underlying fundamental factors.

P&S statement. *See* Purchase and sale statement.

Par—A particular price, 100 percent of principal value.

Parity—A theoretically equal relationship between farm product prices and all other prices. In farm program legislation, parity is defined in such a manner that the purchasing power of a unit of an agricultural commodity is maintained at its level during an earlier historical base period.

Pit—A specially constructed arena on the trading floor of some exchanges where trading in a futures or options contract is conducted by open outcry. On other exchanges, the term "ring" designates the trading area for a futures or options contract.

Point—The minimum fluctuation in futures prices or options premiums.

Point balance—A statement prepared by futures commission merchants to show profit or loss on all open contracts by computing them to an official closing or settlement price.

Pool. *See* Commodity pool.

Position—A market commitment. For example, a buyer of futures contracts is said to have a long position and, conversely, a seller of futures contracts is said to have a short position.

Position limit—The maximum number of futures contracts in certain regulated commodities that one can hold, according to the provisions of the CFTC Reference Reporting Limits.

Position trader—A commodity trader who either buys or sells contracts and holds them for an extended period of time, as distinguished from the day trader, who will normally initiate and liquidate a futures position within a single trading session.

Post-Modern Portfolio Theory—A variation of Modern Portfolio Theory using asymmetrical risk evaluation, as opposed to symmetrical risk evaluation.

Premium—(1) The additional payment allowed by exchange regulations for delivery or higher-than-required standards or grades of a commodity against a futures contract. In speaking of price relationships between different delivery months of a given commodity, one is said to be trading at a premium over another when its price is greater than that of the other; (2) also can mean the amount paid a grantor or writer of an option by a trader.

Price limit—Maximum price advance or decline from the previous day's settlement price permitted for a commodity in one trading session by the rules of the exchange.

Primary markets—The principal market for the purchase and sale of a cash commodity.

Principal—Refers to a person that is a principal of a particular entity; (1) Any person including, but not limited to a sole proprietor, general partner, officer or director, or person occupying a similar status or performing similar functions, having the power, directly or indirectly, through agreement or otherwise, to exercise a controlling influence over the activities of the entity; (2) any holder or any beneficial owner of 10 percent or more of the outstanding shares of any class of stock of the entity; (3) any person who has contributed 10 percent or more of the capital of the entity.

Private wires—Wires leased by various firms and news agencies for the transmission of information to branch offices and subscriber clients.

Proceeding clerk—The member of the commission's staff in the Office of Proceedings who maintains the commission's reparations docket, assigns reparation cases to an appropriate CFTC official, and acts as custodian of the records of proceedings.

Producer—A person or entity that produces (grows, mines, etc.) a commodity.

Public elevators—Grain storage facilities, licensed and regulated by state and federal agencies, in which space is rented out to whomever is willing to pay for it; some are also approved by the commodity exchanges for delivery of commodities against futures contracts.

Purchase and sale statement (P&S)—A statement sent by a commission house to a customer when a futures or options position has been liquidated or offset. The statement shows the number of contracts bought or sold, the gross profit or loss, the commission charges, and the net profit or loss on the transaction; sometimes combined with a confirmation statement.

Purchase price—The total actual cost paid by a person for entering into a commodity option transaction, including premium, commission, or any other direct or indirect charges.

Put (option)—An option that gives the option buyer the right but not the obligation to sell the underlying futures contract at a particular price on or before a particular date.

Pyramiding—The use of profits on existing futures positions as margins to increase the size of the position, normally in successively smaller increments; such as the use of profits on the purchase of five futures contracts as margin to purchase an additional four contracts, whose profits will in turn be used to margin an additional three contracts.

Quotation—The actual price or the bid or ask price of either cash commodities or futures or options contracts at a particular time; often called quote.

R-square—The square of the correlation coefficient. It is the percentage of the variance in two variables explained by the relationship between them. If two CTAs have a correlation coefficient of 0.80, 64 percent of their variation is explained by their relationship.

Rally—An upward movement of prices. *See also* Recovery.

Rally top—The point where a rally stalls. A bull move will usually make several rally tops over its life.

Range—The difference between the high and low price of a commodity during a given period, usually a single trading session.

Reaction—A short-term countertrend movement of prices.

Receivership—A situation in which a receiver has been appointed. A receiver is a person appointed by a court to take custody and control of, and manage the property or funds of, another, pending judicial action concerning them.

Recovery—An upward movement of prices following a decline.

Registered commodity representative (RCR). *See* Associated person (AP); Broker.

Regulations (CFTC)—The regulations adopted and enforced by the federal overseer of futures markets, the Commodity Futures Trading Commission, in order to administer the Commodity Exchange Act.

Reparations—Compensation payable to a wronged party in a futures or options transaction. The term is used in conjunction with the

Commodity Futures Trading Commission's customer claims procedure to recover civil damages.

Reparations award—The amount of monetary damages a respondent may be ordered to pay to a complainant.

Reporting limit—Sizes of positions set by the exchange and/or by the CFTC at or above which commodity traders must make daily reports to the exchange and/or the CFTC as to the size of the position by commodity, by delivery month, and according to the purpose of trading, i.e., speculative or hedging.

Resistance—The price level where a trend stalls; the opposite of a support level. Prices must build momentum to move through resistance.

Respondents—The individuals or firms against which the complaint is filed and a reparations award is sought.

Retender—The right of holders of futures contracts who have been tendered a delivery notice through the clearinghouse to offer the notice for sale on the open market, liquidating their obligation to take delivery under the contract; applicable only to certain commodities and only within a specified period of time.

Retracement—A price movement in the opposite direction of the prevailing trend. *See* Correction.

Ring—A circular area on the trading floor of an exchange where traders and brokers stand while executing futures or options trades. Some exchanges use pits rather than rings.

Risk-reward ratio—An estimation of the amount of potential risk on a particular trade to the amount of potential reward.

Round lot—A quantity of a commodity equal in size to the corresponding futures contract for the commodity, as distinguished from a job lot, which may be larger or smaller than the contract.

Round turn—The combination of an initiating purchase or sale of a futures contract and offsetting sale or purchase of an equal number of futures contracts to the same delivery month. Commission fees for commodity transactions cover the round turn.

Rules (NFA)—The standards and requirements to which participants who are required to be members of National Futures Association must subscribe and conform.

Sample grade—In commodities, usually the lowest quality acceptable for delivery in satisfaction of futures contracts. *See* Contract grades.

Scalper—A speculator on the trading floor of an exchange who buys and sells rapidly, with small profits or losses, holding positions for only a short time during a trading session. Typically, a scalper will stand ready to buy at a fraction below the last transaction price and to sell at a fraction above, thus creating market liquidity.

Seat—Denotes membership on an exchange.

Security deposit. *See* Margin.

Segregated account—A special account used to hold and separate customers' assets from those of the broker or firm.

Selling hedge—Selling futures contracts to protect against possible decreased prices of commodities that will be sold in the future. *See* Hedging; Short hedge.

Semivariance—The variance observed on one side of the mean or a chosen target, measuring volatility of the downside of the mean or the target.

Settlement price—The closing price, or a price within the range of closing prices, which is used as the official price in determining net gains or losses at the close of each trading session.

Short—One who has sold a cash commodity or a commodity futures contract, in contrast to a long, who has bought a cash commodity or futures contract.

Short hedge—Selling futures to protect against possible decreasing prices of commodities. *See also* Hedging.

Slippage—Difference between the theoretical gross price on a trade and the actual; accounts for poor fills, commissions, fees, etc.

Speculator—One who attempts to anticipate commodity price changes and make profits through the sale and/or purchase of commodity futures contracts. A speculator with a forecast of advancing prices hopes to profit by buying futures contracts and then liquidating the obligation to take delivery with a later sale of an equal number of futures of the same delivery month at a higher price. A speculator with a forecast of declining prices hopes to profit by selling commodity futures contracts and then covering the obligation to deliver with a later purchase of futures at a lower price.

Spot—Market for the immediate delivery of the product and immediate payment. May also refer to the nearest delivery month of a futures contract.

Spot commodity. *See* Cash commodity.

Spread (or straddle)—The purchase of one futures delivery month against the sale of another futures delivery month of the same commodity; the purchase of one delivery month of one commodity against the sale of the same delivery month of a different commodity; or the purchase of one commodity in one market against the sale of that commodity in another market, to take advantage of and profit from the distortions from the normal price relationships that sometimes occur. The term is also used to refer to the difference between the price of one futures month and the price of another month of the same commodity. *See also* Arbitrage.

Stop loss—A risk management technique used to close out a losing position at a given point. *See* Stop order.

Stop order—An order that becomes a market order when a particular price level is reached. A sell stop is placed below the market; a buy stop is placed above the market; sometimes referred to as a stop loss order.

Strike price. *See* Exercise price.

Support—A price level at which a declining market has stopped falling; opposite of a resistance price range. Once this level is reached, the market trades sideways for a period of time.

Swaps—An exchange of obligations between two or more entities. Common swaps involve interest rates, currencies, or loans.

Switch—Liquidation of a position in one delivery month of a commodity and simultaneous initiation of a similar position in another delivery month of the same commodity. When used by hedgers, this tactic is referred to as "rolling forward" the hedge.

Symmetrical risk evaluation—Uses standard deviation to measure risk, which is symmetrically distributed around the mean.

Technical analysis—An approach to analysis of futures markets and anticipated future trends of commodity prices. It examines the technical factors of market activity. Technicians normally examine patterns of price range, rates of change, and changes in volume of trading and open interest. These data are often charted to show trends and formations, which serve as indicators of likely future price movements.

Tender—The act on the part of the seller of futures contracts of giving notice to the clearinghouse that he or she intends to deliver the physical commodity in satisfaction of the futures contract. The clearinghouse in turn passes along the notice to oldest buyer of record in that delivery month of the commodity. *See also* Retender.

Tick—Refers to a change in price up or down. *See also* Point.

Ticker tape—A continuous paper tape transmission of commodity or security prices, volume, and other trading and market information, which operates on private or leased wires by the exchanges, available to their member firms and other interested parties on a subscription basis.

Time value—Any amount by which an option premium exceeds the option's intrinsic value.

To-arrive contract—A type of deferred shipment in which the price is based on delivery at the destination point and the seller pays the freight in shipping it to that point.

Traders—(1) People who trade for their own account; (2) employees of dealers or institutions who trade for their employer's account.

Trading range—An established set of price boundaries, with a high price and a low price that a market will spend a marked period of time within.

Transferable notice. *See* Retender.

Trendline—A line drawn that connects either a series of highs or lows in a trend. The trendline can represent either support, as in an uptrend line, or resistance, as in a downtrend line. Consolidations are marked by horizontal trendlines.

Unauthorized trading—Purchase or sale of commodity futures or options for a customer's account without the customer's permission.

Underlying futures contract—The specific futures contract that the option conveys the right to buy (in the case of a call) or sell (in the case of a put).

Uptrend—The gradual movement of prices higher.

Variable limit—A price system that allows price movements for larger than normally allowed price movements under certain conditions. In periods of extreme volatility, some exchanges permit trading and price levels to exceed regular daily limits. At such times, margins may be automatically increased.

Variation margin call—A midseason call by the clearinghouse on a clearing member, requiring the deposit of additional funds to bring clearing margin monies up to minimum levels in relation to changing prices and the clearing member's net position.

Volatility—A measure of a commodity or stock's tendency to move up and down in price, usually based on its daily price history over a period of time.

Volume of trade—The number of contracts traded during a specified period of time.

Warehouse receipt—Document guaranteeing the existence and availability of a given quantity and quality of a commodity in storage; commonly used as the instrument of transfer of ownership in both cash and futures transactions.

Whipsaw—A price pattern characterized by violent moves up and down. A trader gets caught on the wrong side of the market and reverses his or her position, only to get caught again on the wrong side.

Wirehouse. *See* Futures commission merchant (FCM).

Write. *See* Grantor.

Note: This glossary is included to assist the reader in understanding the text of this book and other aspects of the managed futures industries. It is not a legal dictionary, nor a guide to interpreting any security law, state-federal regulations, or any other legal instrument. For legal assistance, be sure to contact your attorney.

D

Top CTA Performers

Top 20 CTA Performers 1994

For the period 1/1/94 to 3/31/94. Includes only CTAs managing at least $1 million as of 3/31/94.*

Trading Advisors	1994 YTD Return	Sterling Ratio	Largest Draw Down	Starting Date	Best 12-Mo. Period	Worst 12-Mo. Period	Funds Under Mgmt
1. International Arbitrage Assoc.	52.66%	0.68	36%	11/88	83%	-21%	$3M
2. Blue Ridge Trading, Ltd.	42.26%	NA	28%	5/92	31%	-5%	$1M
3. Simons Capital, Inc. (Financial)	33.31%	0.83	26%	6/90	52%	-2%	$5M
4. MarketVest, Inc.	32.87%	NA	16%	4/92	63%	11%	$1M
5. Dominick & Dominick Futures, Inc.	19.10%	NA	17%	8/92	34%	-6%	$1M
6. GNI Limited (Spread)	18.24%	1.35	27%	1/86	73%	-8%	$105M
7. HB Capital Management, Inc.	17.32%	0.30	59%	7/90	70%	-44%	$1M
8. James G. Murray, III, CTA	16.55%	0.51	47%	5/87	53%	-40%	$1M
9. GNI Limited (Directional)	14.93%	NA	8%	8/92	60%	37%	$85M
10. Fairfield Financial Group, Inc.	14.86%	0.44	29%	3/82	24%	-29%	$3M
11. Anglo-Dutch Investments (Energy)	14.16%	-0.36	36%	9/85	111%	-26%	$2M
12. ELM Financial, Inc. (Financial)	13.74%	0.61	41%	2/84	81%	-33%	$65M
13. Quest Trading, Inc.	13.23%	0.51	25%	10/89	61%	-17%	$1M
14. Neiderhoffer Investments, Inc.	12.57%	0.46	23%	1/87	43%	-21%	$10M
15. Eclipse Capital Mgmt. (Global Yield)	12.53%	1.01	20%	11/90	48%	-1%	$10M
16. FX 500, Ltd. (Hedge Plus)	12.50%	0.35	24%	4/90	31%	-20%	$87M
17. Robert M. Tamiso & Assoc. (Kintyre)	11.85%	NA	13%	8/91	56%	12%	$7M
18. Toron Capital Management, Inc.	10.90%	NA	10%	7/91	53%	7%	$1M
19. Pecos Management Corp. (Domestic)	10.80%	0.00	30%	8/90	50%	-20%	$3M
20. Loran Futures, Inc. (A-Leg)	10.58%	1.92	16%	11/89	87%	7%	$20M

NOTE*: Performance statistics, except for 1994 Return, are based upon the past 5 years performance or the CTA's entire history, whichever is shorter.

Barclay Trading Group, Ltd., Fairfield, Iowa

Top 20 CTA Performers Past Three Years

For the period 4/1/91 to 3/31/94. Includes only CTAs managing at least $1 million as of 3/31/94.

Trading Advisors	3-Yr Comp. Annual Return	Sterling Ratio	Largest Draw Down	% Qtrs in Top Quartile	Best 12-Mo. Period	Worst 12-Mo. Period	Funds Under Mgmt
1. Darby Trading Consultants, Inc.	86.67%	2.45	40.37%	64%	+275%	+13%	$5M
2. Hasenbichler Commodities AG	62.19%	2.76	18.97%	64%	+163%	+25%	$54M
3. Leboz Trading Company	50.48%	1.59	27.48%	73%	+111%	+13%	$3M
4. Michael J. Frischmeyer, CTA	43.60%	2.00	23.08%	55%	+304%	-7%	$9M
5. Hawksbill Capital (Global Divers.)	40.27%	0.77	35.09%	45%	+196%	-21%	$129M
6. Fort Management, Inc.	39.41%	2.96	3.88%	73%	+71%	+7%	$14M
7. Range Wise, Inc.	37.17%	2.54	6.62%	64%	+89%	+8%	$82M
8. Kelly Valentine & Associates	36.83%	1.46	27.64%	64%	+174%	-28%	$5M
9. Clarke Capital Management, Inc.	34.79%	2.63	38.88%	45%	+271%	-35%	$3M
10. Dunn Capital Mgmt. (TOPS-Fin)	32.33%	1.82	18.16%	36%	+111%	-1%	$112M
11. Thomas D. Reynolds	31.86%	1.76	12.03%	55%	+82%	+11%	$2M
12. Brandywine Asset Mgmt. (Bench.)	31.78%	1.44	18.97%	55%	+79%	+11%	$25M
13. Loran Futures, Inc. (A-Leg)	31.45%	1.92	15.73%	55%	+87%	+7%	$20M
14. Simons Capital, Inc. (Financial)	29.76%	0.83	26.44%	55%	+52%	-2%	$5M
15. HB Capital Management, Inc.	29.62%	0.30	17.46%	36%	+70%	-4%	$1M
16. International Arbitrage Assoc.	29.57%	0.68	25.09%	18%	+74%	+2%	$3M
17. Willowbridge Associates (Titan)	29.41%	0.82	29.90%	64%	+140%	-13%	$13M
18. Wizard Trading, Inc. (Financial)	29.38%	NA	20.33%	64%	+88%	+9%	$2M
19. Three Crown Capital Partners	28.70%	0.88	19.58%	45%	+84%	+0%	$1M
20. Golden Mountain Trading, Inc.	28.53%	1.11	16.57%	55%	+92%	+5%	$57M

Barclay Trading Group, Ltd., Fairfield, Iowa

Top 20 CTA Performers Past Five Years

For the period 4/1/89 to 3/31/94. Includes only CTAs managing at least $1 million as of 3/31/94.

Trading Advisors	5-Yr Comp. Annual Return	Sterling Ratio	Largest Draw Down	% Qtrs in Top Quartile	Best 12-Mo. Period	Worst 12-Mo. Period	Funds Under Mgmt
1. Hawksbill Capital (Global Divers.)	63.12%	0.77	61.82%	53%	+822%	-60%	$129M
2. Capital Futures Mgmt. S.N.C.	60.65%	1.91	18.36%	53%	+232%	+1%	$75M
3. Sjo Asset Mgmt. (Foreign Fin.)	38.17%	1.94	17.33%	47%	+161%	-3%	$166M
4. GNI Limited (Spread)	33.95%	1.35	27.31%	58%	+73%	-8%	$105M
5. Golden Mountain Trading, Inc.	31.76%	1.11	26.63%	47%	+127%	-18%	$57M
6. FX Concepts, Inc. (7:1 Leverage)	31.58%	1.21	22.99%	53%	+116%	-12%	$2,163M
7. Abraham Trading Company	28.87%	0.51	31.96%	47%	+192%	-21%	$49M
8. Pragma, Inc. (Beta)	26.71%	0.40	23.51%	37%	+98%	-13%	$36M
9. Range Wise, Inc.	26.35%	2.54	28.47%	53%	+94%	-19%	$82M
10. Willowbridge Associates (Vulcan)	26.15%	0.86	30.19%	42%	+72%	-15%	$50M
11. Rabar Market Research	24.86%	0.46	27.75%	53%	+174%	-25%	$114M
12. Chescor, Ltd. (Regular)	24.82%	1.42	14.18%	47%	+62%	0%	$110M
13. Friedberg Commodity (Currency)	24.13%	-0.21	58.92%	47%	+414%	-54%	$29M
14. Chesapeake Capital (Diversified)	23.91%	1.32	20.58%	42%	+91%	-9%	$385M
15. Wessex Fund Management Ltd.	23.17%	1.37	5.85%	21%	+74%	+4%	$60M
16. Reynwood Trading Corp. (Curr.)	22.36%	0.59	15.70%	32%	+76%	-15%	$59M
17. Willowbridge Associates (Argo)	21.76%	0.93	21.30%	47%	+71%	-8%	$27M
18. Blenheim Investments, Inc.	21.59%	0.79	16.62%	47%	+66%	-13%	$351M
19. Red Oak Commodity Advisors	21.34%	0.30	20.19%	32%	+89%	-7%	$67M
20. Fenchurch Capital Mgmt., Ltd.	20.26%	1.71	6.48%	32%	+34%	+9%	$476M

Barclay Trading Group, Ltd., Fairfield, Iowa

Top Most Profitable CTAs for the Past Three Years

Ranked by largest cumulative *Net Trading Profts* from 1991 through 1993 with respect to the average amount of *Net Assets* being managed.

CTAs Managing over $10 Million			CTAs Managing under $10 Million		
Advisor Name	**% Return on Equity**	**Net Profit (Millions $)**	**Advisor Name**	**% Return on Equity**	**Net Profit (Millions $)**
1. Eckhardt Trading Company	108.2	16.8	1. Telesis Mgmt. (Leveraged)	183.7	1.0
2. Hawksbill (Global Div.)	92.4	37.6	2. Clarke Capital Mgmt.	153.8	0.3
3. Golden Mountain Trading	82.8	35.0	3. Brandywine (Financial)	115.4	1.1
4. Chescor Limited (High Beta)	77.8	3.5	4. Tommy Reynolds	95.3	0.5
5. Chesapeake Cap. (Diversified)	76.3	113.9	5. Brandywine (Stock Index)	86.2	0.5
6. Fenchurch Capital Mgmt.	73.7	88.8	6. Beacon Mgmt. (Currency)	68.6	0.4
7. Eclipse Cap. (Global Monetary)	71.8	16.1	7. Tactical Investment (Flagship)	65.6	2.3
8. Brandywine (Benchmark)	66.2	1.6	8. Dunn Capital (D-TOPS)	61.5	1.1
9. Willowbridge (Argo)	65.9	10.7	9. Court Master (Metals)	58.8	0.4
10. Dunn Capital (F-TOPS)	65.2	22.3	10. SCI Capital Mgmt.	58.7	2.0
11. Willowbridge (Vulcan)	65.0	30.8	11. Brandywine (Fin. Conservative)	58.1	2.8
12. Sabre Fund Mgmt. (Financial)	60.9	28.6	12. New Forest Capital Mgmt.	57.2	2.2
13. Abraham Trading Co.	56.8	12.2	13. Bonanza Capital Mgmt.	54.8	0.6
14. RxR, Inc. (Fin. Fut.)	56.6	8.5	14. Beacon Mgmt. (Balanced)	51.4	0.5
15. LaSalle Port. (Int'l Cross)	54.9	18.3	15. Murray Investment Company	47.1	0.7
16. Silver Knight Inv. Mgmt.	54.3	6.9	16. Wizard Trading (Diversified)	38.7	0.9
17. Loran Futures, Inc.	53.8	9.5	17. Beacon Mgmt. (Stock)	33.8	0.3
18. PRAGMA, Inc. (Gamma Method)	52.1	9.2	18. TrendLogic (Currency)	31.2	0.6
19. Mark J. Walsh & Co.	47.3	12.3	19. YieldMaster (Eurodollar)	28.3	0.7
20. RxR, Inc. (Mark III)	46.0	28.8	20. Telesis Mgmt. (Institutional)	25.4	0.7
21. Light Blue Trading Ltd.	44.1	2.8	21. QuickSilver Trading Inc.	24.9	0.4
22. D.W. Fut. & Cur. Mgmt. (Div.)	43.4	45.9	22. Commodity Monitors (Financial)	24.6	0.1
23. PRAGMA, Inc. (Beta Method)	41.6	16.5	23. TimeTech Management	20.6	1.9
24. ELM Financial, Inc.	41.4	20.8	24. Gill Capital Mgmt. (Diversified)	19.2	0.4
25. EMC Capital Management	39.2	33.7	25. TrendLogic (Fin. & Metals)	18.6	0.8
26. Visioneering R&D Co. (V-50F)	39.2	3.4	26. Sage Group, Inc.	17.8	1.0
27. Dunn Capital (WMA)	38.7	59.3	27. Jones Commodities (Liquid)	16.7	1.7
28. Sunrise Comm. (CIMCOs)	35.8	9.7	28. Niederhoffer Investments	14.4	1.1
29. Millburn (Global Fin.)	35.0	89.9	29. Parthenon Futures Management	11.0	0.1
30. Rabar Market Research	34.3	23.6	30. Court Master (Basic)	10.1	0.4
Total Net Profits		$817.1	Total Net Profits		$27.3

CTA Equity based performance statistics are exclusively compiled by Stark Research Incorporated. These statistics are developed from information obtained directly from the individual CTAs. While the information is believed to be reliable, because of the complexities involved with the data and the fact that it has not been verified, we cannot guarantee its completeness or accuracy. Reproduction without written permission is strictly forbidden.

Index